T0166388

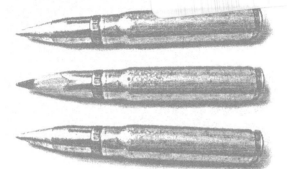

Also by Farzana Marie:

POETRY
Letters to War and Lethe (2014)

NONFICTION
Hearts for Sale! A Buyer's Guide to Winning in Afghanistan (2013)

LOAD POEMS LIKE GUNS

Women's Poetry from Herat, Afghanistan

Compiled, Translated, Introduced by

FARZANA MARIE

Foreword by

DR. SHARIF FAYEZ

Holy Cow! Press
Duluth, Minnesota
2015

First printing, 2015

ISBN 978-0-9859818-8-4

10 9 8 7 6 5 4 3 2 1

This project is supported in part by grant awards from the Ben and
Jeanne Overman Charitable Trust, the Elmer L. and Eleanor J. Andersen
Foundation, the Cy and Paula DeCosse Fund of the Minneapolis Foun-
dation, and by gifts from individual donors.

HOLY COW! PRESS books are distributed to the trade by Consortium
Book Sales & Distribution, c/o Perseus Distribution, 1094 Flex Drive,
Jackson, TN 38301.

For inquiries, please write to: HOLY COW! PRESS, Post Office Box 3170,
Mount Royal Station, Duluth, MN 55803.
www.holycowpress.org

For Nadia Anjuman
and Afghanistan's women poets

TABLE OF CONTENTS

FOREWORD   IX

TRANSLITERATION SYSTEM   XII

PREFACE   XV

ACKNOWLEDGMENTS   XIX

INTRODUCTION

     Why Poetry? Why Herat?   1

     Herat: A Brief History   6

     Nadia Anjuman: Sketch of Her Life and Work   13

GENERAL NOTE ON THE TRANSLATIONS   31

NADIA ANJUMAN   35

     Makes No Sense   38

     Mountain, Sea   40

     My Garden   42

     Divine Beauty   44

     Smoke-Bloom   46

MUZHGAN FARAMANESH   49

     Ghazal 1   52

     Ghazal 2   54

     Quatrain 1   56

     Quatrain 2   58

     Quatrain 3   60

     Quatrain 4   62

FARIBA HAIDARI   65

     Odor of Death   68

     A Young Street-Vendor Thinks of Imported Goods   74

     And Violet Tunes of Lawlessness   78

NILUFAR NIKSEAR   85

     Ghazal 1   88

     At Night in This Empty Neighborhood   90

     Ghazal 2   92

     Ghazal 3   94

FERESHTA NILAB SAHEL NOORZAYI   97
    But I Couldn't   100
    These Days   102
    Sincerity   104
    Red Line   106
    Farewell   108

SOMAIA RAMISH   111
    The Girl Who Sold God   114
    And the Word Null   116
    Another Looking Glass, Another Lie   118
    Load Poems like Guns   120
    For Nadia Anjuman   122

ELAHA SAHEL   125
    Sinful Skirts   128
    Ode to My Earrings   130
    Rows of Pockmarked Homes   132
    Didn't He Come Home?   134
    A Canvas   136
    Protest   138

ROYA SHARIFI   145
    A Gamble   148
    Fragrance of Dreams   150
    Those Bleeding Tulips   152

SELECTED BIBLIOGRAPHY   155
ABOUT THE AUTHOR   163

FOREWORD

THIS BOOK INTRODUCES eight leading Herati women poets, with a selection of their poems in translation along with the original Persian Dari. It starts with a long introduction, which provides some remarkable historical, cultural, and geopolitical facts on Herat and its literary legacy. In addition, the biographical sketches on the poets selected for this project offer some revealing information about their literary works, poetic themes, styles, and visions. For some contemporary Afghan poets, modern poetry has often meant ambiguity and some of that exists in these poems, but the author has tried to deal with this problem in an effective way in her translations.

In her introduction, Farzana Marie explains that despite recurrent invasions and wars, such as the Taliban's most repressive rule and cultural vandalism, Herat has continued to maintain its historical mission as a seat of culture and arts in the region over the centuries. With democracy being institutionalized in the country, educated women in Afghanistan, particularly in Herat, have begun to use new and traditional ways of expression to promote and protect their human rights. In Herat—as in Kabul and elsewhere—poetry, with its symbolic language, is being explored and effectively used as a powerful means of protest against gender discrimination and injustice. Some young female artists in Herat have also turned to making short films dealing with social and political issues, particularly domestic violence against women.

A major part of the introduction is about the rise of Nadia Anjuman as a new star in the artistic city of Herat, her painful struggle to gain artistic recognition as a leading female poet, her forced unhappy marriage, and her tragic death at the hands of her husband. Out of this tragic death, Nadia, like Rābia Balkhī and Gauharshād, emerges as an iconic symbol for the cause of her oppressed gender. Farzana explains that Nadia has also become a source of inspiration and spiritual power for younger female poets struggling to express, through art, their resistance to the injustices of their male-dominated society. She demonstrates that poetry, as a result of this tragedy, has also emerged as a more powerful means of communicating, perpetuating, and universalizing the cause of Afghan women in their battle against gender discrimination and domestic violence. Farzana Marie brings these issues to life through a critical examination of Nadia's works as well as interviews with her friends and relatives.

What distinguishes this introductory study from similar attempts in the past is the author's direct and profound knowledge of the subject, as reflected in the introduction, which illustrates how the rich literary heritage of Herat, with its strong tradition of tolerance and resilience, has enabled Nadia and her fellow poets to continue their education and continue to write poetry even during the most dreadful reign of the Taliban when women were completely banned from attending public and private schools. Shedding light on the creative means by which they accomplished this, the introduction also provides fascinating information about how a number of academics, led by Professor Naser Rahyab of Herat University, set up a secret literary club called the Golden Needle, providing young poets and writers a place to discuss important literary works and craft their own writing during the Taliban's repressive rule.

Written with candor and compassion, the introduction will also inspire young Afghan readers, who may have little access to such analytical works on modern Dari poetry. Furthermore, a study of this nature on a most sensitive issue—domestic violence against women—will be received as a message of hope and encouragement by the educated women of Afghanistan that they can use arts, particularly poetry, as an effective means of expressing and promoting their cause within their society and the international community.

In the second part of the book, the author presents in English translation a selection of poems from Nadia Anjuman, Muzhgan Faramanesh, Fariba Haidari, Nilufar Niksear, Fereshta Nilab Sahel Noorzayi, Somaia Ramish, Roya Sharifi, and Elaha Sahel. These poems teem with images of hope, despair, unfulfilled desires, and dreams. Although the threat of the return of the Taliban has receded, women in Afghanistan, particularly the intellectual ones, are still confronting red lines wherever they go, as Nilab Sahel says in her poem "Red Line":

Why, oh why
would you step on this red line
demarking precipice?
Pull your foot away—quick!
Lest the abyss
erase you.

—*Dr. Sharif Fayez*
Professor and Founding President
American University of Afghanistan

TRANSLITERATION SYSTEM

This book uses a simplified system close to the IJMES (International Journal of Middle East Studies) transliteration system for Persian. The major difference, employed to make the text more readable, is the absence of special designations for different letters representing extremely similar and sometimes indistinguishable sounds. For instance, in Persian there are three different letters giving an "s" sound, and these are simply represented with an s rather than distinguishing between the Persian/Dari letters with permutations like ṣ. The simplified transliteration chart follows a short list of exceptions.

Exceptions to the transliteration system:

- In the spelling of names, the manuscript reflects the preferred English spelling, if any, used by poets, interviewees, authors, or others.

- For readability, the transliterated pronunciation of each poet's name is given only once, at the beginning of her biographical note.

- Where the Persian word or name has a standard English equivalent, it is used; for instance, country and city names like "Afghanistan" and "Herat."

- Where the term or name comes from another source, such as in a footnote, it is preserved as spelled in the original.

CONSONANTS

ء	’	ص	s
ب	b	ض	z
پ	p	ط	t
ت	t	ظ	z
ث	s	ع	‘
ج	j	غ	gh
چ	ch	ف	f
ح	h	ق	q
خ	kh	ک	k
د	d	گ	g
ذ	z	ل	l
ر	r	م	m
ز	z	ن	n
ژ	zh	ه	h
س	s	و	w *or* u
ش	sh	ي	y

VOWELS

Long	ا	ā
	و	ū
	ى	ī
Doubled, final form	ى	iyy
	و	uww
Diphthongs	وَ	au
	ىَ	ai
Short	ــَ	a
	ــُ	u
	ــِ	i *or* e

PREFACE

THE NAME OF Afghanistan's third-largest city evokes a parade of colorful images: Deep lapis-blue handcrafted glass. Parapets of a sand-hued citadel. Pine-lined avenues. A 600-year-old minaret with a rocket-sized wound. Poetry recitations with language flowing like wine. That's Herat. A city with grandeur and struggle in its past, a question mark in its future, and a battle for identity in the middle. And one of the most vivid battlegrounds for this struggle—where its skirmishes are recorded as well as fought—is contemporary literature.

The entrance to Herat's Literary Society (*Anjuman-e Adabīy-e Herat*) is unassuming, set back from the honk-happy main street just east of Cinema Square (*Chawk-e Cīnemā*), where a giant flashing TV screen and dozens of billboards jostle for eye-catching corner space. When you want to go there, you ask the taxi driver for *Kitābkhānaye āmeh*, or Herat's public library, a neighboring building to the Literary Society. The sidewalk on either side of the courtyard entrance is lined with bookshops, where colorful shelves and stacks of dusty volumes stretch to the ceiling. Among those books, aided by the eagle-eyed shopkeeper, you will find a variety of short poetry collections by Herati women. It is very likely that among the small stack produced for your perusal will be an edition of Nadia Anjuman's *Gul-e Dudī*, "Smoke-Bloom" (author's rendition).

It was Wednesday afternoon when I ducked between the bookshops, out of the busy street noise. This was Herat Literary Society's designated time for young poets to gather, taking turns to read their latest work aloud and receive critiques as well as affirmation from around the room. I had been invited by Elaha Sahel, one of the regulars, who was eight-and-a-half months pregnant and would not be attending that day. She had apparently called ahead to introduce me because when I arrived, the director, Mr. Wali Shah Bahrah, greeted me warmly and said they were expecting me. There was some time before the workshop session would begin, so I wandered into the small reception room just inside the building's entrance, where I was cheerfully greeted by a young receptionist named Fatima. The room was small but equipped with the essentials: a computer at which Fatima presided, a scanner-printer, bookshelves lining one wall, and a thermos of tea. While the pay was meager (it seems artists the world over have much in common), it was a decent job for Fatima, who studied for her university art classes in between receiving visitors and cataloguing books. On a chair in one corner I noticed a stunning piece of calligraphy, which turned out to be Fatima's, and in the room's opposite corner on the bookshelf stood a single portrait. It was of Nadia Anjuman.

The purpose of my journey to Herat in 2013 was primarily to learn about this Afghan poet, who adopted "Anjuman" for her writing name in honor of the literary society that she loved: *Anjuman-e Adabīy-e Herat*. I knew the essence of Nadia's story, a young woman whose life and writings had clearly left a deep mark on her fellow poets, the literary group, the city of Herat, and the nation as a whole. I knew that the young Herati poet had died in 2005 after an incident of domestic violence and shortly after releasing her first book. I knew that she had left behind a six-month-old child and her death had stunned admirers of her poetry from across the country and beyond. But there was surely more to this story than what had made its way to the headlines and a few scattered websites. And it wasn't just Nadia's story that compelled me to study her work and life—there were many stories like hers, although writers with her talent are rare. Perhaps more importantly, there were many new voices rising to fill the space left by Nadia's silence. This collection seeks to begin listening to those voices.

For me, translation is like a conversation, one that sharpens my own thinking and creative work while inviting new faces to the table of listening. A short poem of my own offers a wish for this translation project and the conversations I hope it will inspire.

So much wrapped
in the gift of a word: *salaam*

Newborn seams close
at birth-opening: your eyes
into mine

[Sand adapts silently]

Let us be more
listen to the soil
than we hold onto:
not like sand but not
like stone.

—*Farzana Marie*

ACKNOWLEDGMENTS

THIS TRANSLATION PROJECT would have been impossible without the assistance and insight of mentors, teachers, and colleagues, and friends. I am indebted to Dr. Sharif Fayez, Dr. Kamran Talattof, Dr. Susan Briante, Dr. Senzil Nawid, Ms. Suraia Ehrari, Mr. Asef Hosseini, Dr. Amin and Mrs. Aqila Rustaqi, and Dr. Emily Hervey for their time and improvements to this manuscript. I am profoundly grateful for the generous support of the Roshan Cultural Heritage Institute, the Dr. Malakeh Taleghani Endowment, the American Institute for Afghanistan Studies, and the Michael E. Bonine Travel and Research Award from the University of Arizona's School of Middle Eastern and North African Studies that made it possible to complete this project.

Yak jahān tashakur (a world of thanks) to poets Elaha Sahel, Somaia Ramish, Fariba Haidari, Roya Sharifi, Muzhgan Faramanesh, and Nilufar Niksear for working with me in person and virtually to enrich my understanding of their poems; and to colleagues in Herat—Mohammad Shafi Noorzayi, Gulsoom Sediqi, Laila Raziqi, Mr. Wali Shah Bahrah and the Herat Literary Society, Dr. Mohammad Naser Rahyab, Dr. Mohammad Dawood Munir, and the Weaver family for their kind hospitality and assistance.

A heartfelt thanks to my family, especially my parents, John and Debbie Hervey, for encouraging my creative spirit and love for other cultures and languages since my earliest days.

I thank God for the gifts and opportunities to be involved in this moving work and the strength to pursue it.

INTRODUCTION
WHY POETRY? WHY HERAT?

Khorasan is the oyster shell of the world,
and Herat is its pearl.
—Ancient Proverb

THIS COLLECTION OFFERS a focused selection of post-2001 Herati women's poetry in translation. I begin with an explanation of the reasons for the chosen timeframe, gender-specificity, literary form, and especially the region's unique importance to the intellectual landscape of Afghanistan. First, the choice to focus on women's poetry, rather than a broader selection of work by both male and female poets, is closely connected to the timeframe. The history of female poets in the land now known as Afghanistan is a rich one, with famous examples going as far back as Rābi'a Balkhī of the 10th century. We learn from the work of more recent poetesses like Āisha Durrānī in the 19th century that writing poetry was fairly unusual, though not impossible, for women of her time. Still, literary activities were usually limited to the wealthy or those in powerful positions.

Outside of Afghanistan, there is some, albeit limited, access to the work of female Afghan poets who wrote toward the middle and latter part of the 20th century (some of whom are still writing), like Bahar Saeed, Nadia Fazl, Parwin Pazhkwak, and others. In the years following the serial conflicts that began with the Soviet invasion of 1979, the vast majority of these poets were uprooted from their homeland and took refuge in far-flung countries including the

U.K., the U.S., Germany, Denmark, the Netherlands, and Canada, along with Iran, India, and Pakistan. Many continued to write, and are still living and writing in these countries today, with especially vibrant poetic communities in Europe and Iran.[1]

This exodus led to the creation of a body of Afghan literature by both men and women in exile, which is acquiring a unique space and voice of its own. While the spectrum of work available is still extremely limited, speakers of English and European languages have relatively greater access to the work of diaspora writers than of those still living in Afghanistan. Potential translators have greater access to work written in Dari or Pashto, such as that of Shakila Azizzada and Reza Mohammadi (a male poet), whose poetry has been beautifully translated into English by the Poetry Translation Centre in London.[2] I have located two slim volumes[3] of Afghan women's Dari poetry in English translation, mostly containing older writing or works of diaspora poets. Afghan writers are also beginning to produce work in the languages of the countries where they reside, especially second-generation writers. For instance, Zohra Saed and Sahar Muradi recently compiled and edited a fine collection by Afghan American writers, called *One Story, Thirty Stories: An Anthology of Contemporary Afghan-American Literature* (University of Arkansas Press, 2010).

---

1   For more on female Afghan poets in Iran, see Anna Vanzan's article, "The Double Exile: The Poetry of Afghan Women Refugees in Iran," *El Ghibli rivista online di letteratura della migrazione* (2008) and Zuzanna Olszeswka "A Desolate Voice: Poetry and Identity among Young Afghan Refugees," *Iranian Studies. Special Issue: Afghan Refugees* 40(2007): 203-224.

2   See their website, www.poetrytranslation.org, which houses a rich archive of contemporary poetry in translation, including the work of several living Afghan poets.

3   Massoud Mirshahi and Leila Enayat-Seraj, *Hidden Face of Afghan Women: Poetess Women of Afghanistan* (Khavaran, 2000) and Shahbaz Ehsani, *Mirrors and Songs: A Selection of Poetry of Afghan Women.* (Self-published, 2012).

These works produced outside Afghanistan offer important insights into a variety of Afghan literary styles, themes, and perspectives. However, access to the work of poets living and writing in Afghanistan is vital to a more complete understanding of contemporary literature. Gaining access to this work is significantly more challenging, since most books in Afghanistan are published locally, making them difficult to find even in other Afghan cities.[4] Many poets are increasingly using Facebook and the Internet to share their poetry, which makes it more accessible, but translations found in online forums (with the exception of quality operations like the Poetry Translation Centre) are often not very high in quality. Some useful nascent resources in English on Afghan literary voices include Aria Fani's blog (Ariafani.com) and the work of journalists like Eliza Griswold and Lyse Doucet.

This collection is a humble effort to begin expanding the availability in English of contemporary Afghan poets in print, facilitating further dialogue and study. The scope is narrow: limited to the work of several contemporary Herati women poets, published post-2001 or post-Taliban. The Taliban regime's restrictions on activities like reading and writing for Afghan women resulted in something of a "blackout" in published work by female poets inside Afghanistan from the mid-1990s through 2001. Women still composed poetry, of course, but it was virtually impossible to publish their work. With women cut off from formal education by an ultra-conservative and discriminatory regime, many—like Nadia Anjuman and her associates—resorted to pursuing their education in secret. Many produced thoughtful, high-quality writing including short stories and poems, refining them in underground workshops or informal gatherings. Unfortunately, most of the work written during this time has not been published, making it much less accessible (although an important area for future study!). While the artistic and publishing environment was also

---

4   For example, books I was able to find and purchase in Herat were not available in Kabul and vice versa.

very restrictive for men during Taliban times, it was immeasurably more so for women. Thus, the post-Taliban writings of women are an especially precious and revealing window into the impact of the years they were "imprisoned" (as many describe it) in their homes and barred from formal education, and their vision of what comes next. The sudden reinstatement of poetry and other artistic forms as possible venues for women's creative public expression after half a dozen years of prohibition makes a study of the work produced in the decade or so that followed particularly meaningful. Taliban-era poems written by Herati women but published later, such as several by Nadia Anjuman, were still considered eligible for this collection.

Studying women's writing in Afghanistan is also significant because of the monumental challenges that remain for those who choose to compose and publish creative work, and the ways that the work itself engages with those very personal struggles as well as the broader socio-political issues. The story of Nadia Anjuman serves as a sobering example of the battles faced by a young female poet, even one with an educated and supportive family in the urban setting of Herat. While her people have working tirelessly toward recovery as a nation since 2001, the future of Afghanistan remains fraught with uncertainty as citizens weather a host of political and economic transitions characterizing the second decade of the 21st century. Dwindling international military support accompanied by reduced development funding, recovering from the debacle of the 2014 presidential election, and potential negotiations with insurgents all bear serious implications for the situation of women in Afghan society. The broad spectrum of emotions, images, and ideas represented in the post-Taliban poetry of Herati women is important for grasping layers of nuance in contemporary societal and gender issues that are often simplified for public consumption.

Why, then, the focus on poetry, and why Herat?

Among the artistic and literary forms, poetry holds an exceedingly revered place in the consciousness of the people of

Afghanistan, not only among its Persian (Dari) speakers,[5] but also among its large Pashto-speaking population (where a major form of oral composition and transmission is the two-line *landay*[6]), as well as other ethnic groups including Hazaras and Uzbeks. While forms and styles differ among Afghanistan's richly diverse population, the broad appeal of poetry as a means of communicating important ideas, passing on stories and heritage, and making political statements, is unmistakable.[7] Part of what has made poetry such an enduring art form despite the many conflicts and upheavals in Afghanistan's history is its orality. While architectural masterpieces, sculptures, paintings, and other physical artifacts could be destroyed, oral forms of transmission and preservation of cultural and literary memory were more difficult to interrupt. The vast majority of Afghans, even those who are illiterate, have a deep appreciation for poetry and most have a colorful variety of poems stored in their memories. Those with even an elementary education will be familiar with classical poets like Mowlānā (Jelālludīn Rumi) and Sa'adī Shirāzī. Afghan women, mostly in Kabul and other large cities, are beginning to gain or regain access to a wide variety of artistic forms, including visual and musical arts, even experimenting with rap music and public graffiti-style art.[8] But the

5   Most Tajiks, Afghanistan's second-largest ethnic group, use Persian. In general, Persian also serves as the common language between ethnic groups in the northern, central, and western parts of the country, whereas Pashto is more predominantly used throughout the South and East.

6   Some helpful English collections of Afghan women's *landay* do exist in English: Sayd Bahodine Majrouh and Marjolijn de Jager's *Songs of Love and War: Afghan Women's Poetry* (Other Press, 2003), the entire June 2013 issue of *Poetry* magazine, and a forthcoming volume from photographer Seamus Murphy and translator Eliza Griswold, *I Am the Beggar of the World: Landays from Contemporary Afghanistan*.

7   For an example, see Partaw Naderi, "Literature in the Course of Politics in Afghanistan." *Tajikam* Website. 2007-2011.

8   For an example, see the profile and work of Shamsia Hassani, a digital and graffiti artist in Kabul on the website www.kabulartproject.com.

power and accessibility of poetry is still very much in its simplicity: all you need to compose is a pen and paper (or if you're not literate, your mind and memory).

The landscape of contemporary poetry in Afghanistan is rich, and getting richer as the country works to recover from decades riddled with conflict and hyper-repression. There is a large concentration of Dari-speaking poets and literary figures in the capital, Kabul, along with other major cities like Mazar-e Sharif and smaller cities like Faizabad in the northern province of Badakhshan, a traditional stronghold of poetry. The city of Herat, however, holds a special position in the country's literary and artistic history, and a sense of that heritage is palpable. There is no doubt about the historical influence of Herati cultural and literary production on the region, and there is every indication that Herat can and will again become a city of deep importance for contemporary Persian and Afghan literature.[9] A study of the poets and poetry of this region, then, is a vital step toward understanding the poetry of Afghanistan as a whole.

HERAT: A BRIEF HISTORY

A brief historical sketch of the city of Herat[10] serves to highlight both the city's deep artistic and literary roots, and the region's extensive suffering through war and conquest, which I argue have

---

9   Due to the nature of Herat's population, which overwhelmingly speaks Persian/Dari, there are few Pashto-language poets in Herat. None of the bookstores I visited in 2013 and 2014 were able to locate any books of poetry by female poets in Pashto, and thus all the work included in this volume was written in Dari.

10   The historical overview included here is very abbreviated and aims to provide a sense of historial elements and events that have most deeply impacted literature and the arts in Herat. This is not intended as a detailed historical study, and there are many excellent resources along those lines. A particularly readable account by Bijan Omrani and Matthew Leeming begins with Herat's ancient history, centuries before Alexander the Great is found in *Afghanistan: A Companion and Guide* (Odyssey Books and Guides, 2005) 305-375.

strengthened the literary community's resolve to hold even more tightly to the heritage of words that cannot be destroyed with tanks or rockets. The historical foundation provides a backdrop for the story of contemporary poets like Nadia Anjuman, whose poems, life, and death have had a profound impact on many poets writing in Herat today. While Anjuman's influence extends much further than Herat, to cities like Kabul and Mazar-Sharif as well as abroad, this collection of writing by Herati women poets consists mainly of those connected to the artistic community that meant so much Nadia. That community revolves, and has revolved for nearly a century, around Herat's Literary Society.

Anjuman-e Adabiy-e Herat, as the organization is called in Dari (the Persian of Afghanistan), is proud to be the oldest literary association in the country, having been established in solar hijri[11] year 1309, or 1930.[12] That was 50 years before the poet Nadia Anjuman was born, which was in the early period of the Soviet occupation,

---

11   The solar hijri calendar system (*hijri shamsi*) is used in Iran and Afghanistan. It is also known as the Persian or Iranian calendar and different from the lunar Muslim (*hijri qamari*) calendar used in most of the rest of the Islamic world. Both Islamic or hijri calendars begin in the year 622 AD, which marks the emigration of the Prophet Mohammad from Mecca to Medina (the original *hajj* or pilgrimage). The solar hijri year begins at the spring equinox (around March 21 of the Gregorian calendar), which is marked by *Nauruz*, the Persian New Year's holiday also celebrated by Turkic peoples throughout Central and Southwest Asia, the Kurdish people, and others.

12   This is the date included in the Literary Society's official logo. According to the Encyclopaedia Iranica, the first official academic and cultural society was established in *Kabul* in 1930 by King Mohammad Nader Shah (who ruled Afghanistan 1929-1933). The entry on "Anjoman-i Adabi" (Literary Society) in Ludwig Adamec's *Historical Dictionary of Afghanistan* does not name a city, but agrees that Nadir Shah established it in 1930. There seems to be a slight discrepancy, however, as Christina Lamb cites an even earlier date in her book, *The Sewing Circles of Herat*. As quoted to her by the society's director Ahmed Said Haghighi, Herat's Anjuman-e Adabī "was founded in 1920 by the poets of the city to make known the rich culture and heritage of Herat" (154).

an especially devastating time in the city of Herat. Kabul was left relatively untouched during the Soviet period; the destruction of Afghanistan's capital city occurred mostly during the civil war of the early 1990s, when various Mujahideen groups were warring for control. Herat was ravaged years earlier, largely as a result of their resistance against the Soviets and the rebellions against occupation. As retribution for an early rebellion with casualties numbering in the hundreds on the Soviet side, airstrikes and artillery killed tens of thousands of Heratis and destroyed ancient landmarks, including several of the minarets belonging to the Musalla complex built in the 15th century.[13]

The Musalla, composed of a mosque, a theological college, and a mausoleum, was the brainchild of one of Afghanistan's most important female leaders and a famous patron of art and literature, Queen Gowharshād—the "Happy Jewel."[14] This art-loving royal lady, wife of Emperor Shāhrukh (Tamerlane's youngest son), is remembered for sponsoring vast architectural projects like the Musalla and for lavishing the court's patronage on painters, calligraphers, poets, and architects, leading many to call the period under her leadership a golden age of art and literature for Herat. Most famously, the painter Behzād and Persian poet Jamī graced the Timurid court, which despite its Chagatai Turkish linguistic ties encouraged the use of Persian. Herat's atmosphere seemed to attract or nurture so many with the artistic flame that 15th century luminary Ali Sher Nawa'i remarked that one could not stretch out a leg in Herat "without poking a poet in the ass."[15]

---

13   The 1400s were considered Herat's "golden age" of art and culture, and as such represent a natural starting point in time for this sketch, even though preceded by various significant events and catasrophes, such as the Mongol invasion of the 13th century.

14   While this is the most commonly used translation of Gowharshād, her name can also mean joyful or happy *essence*.

15   Christina Lamb, *Sewing Circles*, (Perennial, 2002) 153.

Although most of the twenty or more minarets originally located throughout the Musalla grounds have succumbed to various invasions, wars, earthquakes, and the harsh weather and winds of many centuries, five of them remain, stripped of their once-elaborate tiling save for the smattering of stubborn lapis-blue and turquoise-green fragments that yet cling to their sides. These colorful specks nevertheless assist with the imaginative leap required to conjure the image of the queen moving through the courtyards with her entourage, inspecting the projects she had commissioned. Rather shockingly, one of the stories about Queen Gowharshād refers to just such an occasion, when the queen was visiting the Musalla with 200 maidens in her retinue. According to priopriety, the rooms occupied by male seminary students had been vacated prior to her arrival, but one student had been fast asleep and was still in his room. As the legend goes, one of Gowharshād's maidens found the flustered youth in his chamber and the result of their encounter left her disheveled in manner and appearance, leaving no doubt as to what had happened. Rather than punish the young girl, Gowharshād's response was to marry her 200 maidens to the seminary students.[16]

After Shah Rukh's death, the Timurids went through a period of strife, but Herat saw another period of flourishing art and literature in the late 1400s under emperor Sultan Husayn Bayraqa. Himself a writer and poet, Sultan Husayn was also patron to famed miniaturist Bihzād and celebrated Sufi mystic poet Jamī, among other luminaries.[17] Herat figures prominently in the writings of Mogul Emperor Babur, who visited a cousin there in 1506, shortly after Sultan Husyan's death. Babur recounts the decadence he encountered in Herat, even mentioning the musicians and dancers by

---

16   Omrani and Leeming, *Afghanistan: A Companion and Guide* (Odyssey Books and Guides 2005) 332, quoting from travel writings of Mohum Lal (Kashmiri assistant to Sir Alexander Burnes), published in London, 1846. The story is recounted in many places including the article "Gowharshad's Tomb Restored," *Afghan Scene* magazine, July 2013.

17   Omrani and Leeming, *Afghanistan* (Odyssey, 2005) 335.

name ("Hafiz Haji sand well, as Herati people sing, quietly, delicately, and in tune").[18] Husayn's sons, quite literally drunk with pleasure and luxury, ended up incapable of defending the city against the invading Uzbeks, who conquered it within the year.

If the 1400s were a golden age for Herat, during which it enjoyed substantial economic wealth, physical beautification, and a flourishing intellectual and artistic environment (at least at court), the intervening centuries have done much to whittle away at the accomplishments of that era. In 1507, Herat fell to Uzbek invaders from Central Asia, only to be overtaken several years later by Shah Ismail, who would initiate the Safavid dynasty of Persia. During the rest of the 16th and 17th centuries, Herat was neither lavished with the attention and development that it had received under the Timurids, nor plagued with the disastrous incursions that followed. Along with the Persian Savafids, the Mogul empire in India (whose emperor, Babur, had also fallen in love with Kabul), the Uzbek khanate based in Bukhara, the Ottoman Empire, and the emerging Russian Empire kept each other at bay, achieving an overall effect of relative stability. Toward the end of the 16th century, Shah Abbas, who was born in Herat and is considered the greatest of the Safavid rulers, ascended to the throne in Safavid Persia.

It was in the early 1700s that the Safavid Empire began its collapse following the revolt of the Ghilzai tribe in Kandahar and the sacking of Isfahan. Pashtun leader Mirweis Hotak led a revolution gaining the independence of Kandahar province from the Safavids in 1709. After his death, a chaotic time followed, with power shifting among various family members (who repeatedly disposed of each other violently) and complicated by Turks and Russians moving to occupy various parts of Persia. Beginning in 1719, Herat changed hands five times in four decades (between the Hotakis, the Persians, and the Durranis) and was under siege for a total of 24 months.[19]

---

18   Omrani and Leeming, 339.

19   John Carl Nelson, *Thesis: The Siege of Herat 1837-1838* (St. Cloud State University, 1976) Online Edition, chapter 1.

In 1747, Nader Shah, the last-gasp leader of the Safavids, was assassinated by his own guards. Ahmad Shah Durrani (also known as Ahmad Shah Baba and Ahmad Khan Abdali), who had served loyally in Nader Shah's army, marched with his troops back to Kandahar. There, Ahmad Shah was elected leader by a *Loya Jirga* or Grand Council among the confederacy of tribes. He then consolidated territories throughout modern-day Afghanistan and Eastern Iran, including Herat. The Afghan empire was at its largest during the reign of Ahmad Shah, but after his death in 1772 his successors lost control of these far-flung lands.[20]

In the early 1800s, Herat again became the site of conflict with the Persians. After a battle in 1805, Kabul was forced to pay tribute in order to continue governing the city. In 1816, the governor of Mashad advanced on Herat and fought the Afghan army to something of a stalemate (with both sides claiming victory).[21] The city remained under Afghan control, but became the scene of power struggles between different clans of Durrani Pashtuns in the years that followed. While the rise of Dost Mohammad Khan provided a brief semblance of stability, the rivalries continued to tear the country apart, leaving Herat adrift and vulnerable to the incursions of foreign empires, neck-deep in what became known as the Great Game.

Herat's greatest asset—its location—was also its greatest curse. Located in the fertile Hari Rud river valley between mountains and desert, it sat on the main West-East route from the Mediterranean Sea to India or China as well as the major route going north into Central Asia—and Russia. Aside from making the city an economic and cultural hub, Herat's location made it a strategic military asset, one located precisely on Russia's way to British India (or vice versa). In 1838, a Russian-driven Persian

---

20   John Carl Nelson, *The Siege of Herat 1837-1838*, chapter 1. Also see Ganda Singh, *Ahmad Shah Durrani: Father of Modern Afghanistan*. (Bombay: Asia Publishing House, 1959) 24.

21   John Carl Nelson, chapter 2.

invasion of Herat was repelled by the Heratis, with help from various Afghan allies as well as British advances against the Persians.[22] In that same year, British forces moved to invade Afghanistan after its leader, Dost Mohammad Khan, refused to place its foreign relations under British guidance and reached out to Moscow instead. The British invasion that followed included the massacre of their army and thousands of civilian camp followers in 1842.

The Persians besieged Herat yet again in 1856, but were forced to withdraw when the British (now allied with their former enemy, Afghan ruler Dost Mohammad Khan) took the city of Bushire on the Persian Gulf. The battle was renewed a few years later in 1862, resulting in a more decisive victory for the British-Afghan alliance. Herat remained a central strategic concern for British and Russian interests, as evidenced by the publication of books like Charles Marvin's *Russians at the Gates of Herat* (1885). Chapter 5 of that hurriedly and urgently produced volume[23] details "How Herat is the Key of India," and why generals on both sides described it this way. Indeed, since so many natural barriers (like towering mountain ranges) existed between Russia and India on an eastern route—through Kabul—the natural alternative was the western route. The "great midway camping ground" on this route, as described by Marvin, was Herat.[24]

One of the greatest devastations to befall Herat's artistic and architectural heritage occurred in 1885, when the British undertook to "clear" most of the Musalla complex, fearing it would obstruct their line of artillery fire against the advancing Russians, who never came. In fact, the Russians waited ninety-four more years to approach Herat, until the Soviet invasion of 1979. The darkness of the Soviet period, during which thousands were killed

---

22   Peter Hopkirk. "Great Game Timeline," in *The Great Game and Setting the East Ablaze* (Kodansha International, 1995).

23   Marvin, Charles. *Russians at the Gates of Herat*, (Charles Scribner's Sons, 1885), Preface.

24   Marvin, 2.

in a revolt, was dwarfed only by the invasion of the Taliban in 1995 and the years that followed. The Taliban's brand of extremist oppression seemed specially designed to torture the sensitive and poetically inclined people of Herat, attempting to stamp out the very culture and art that formed the core of Herati identity. It was only the Taliban's ignorance and oblivion that provided some saving grace in the midst of this dark period.

NADIA ANJUMAN: SKETCH OF HER LIFE AND WORK

Perhaps all the more because of their troubled history, many in Herat, especially the intellectual and highly educated community, hold tightly to the city's legacy as a cultural and literary center of Afghanistan. "A society needs poets and storytellers to reflect its pain—and joy," mused Herat University Professor Mohammad Naser Rahyab in a 2001 interview with Christina Lamb. "A society without literature is a society that is not rich and does not have a strong core. If there wasn't so much illiteracy...terrorism would never have found its cradle here."[25]

The vast majority of Heratis were appalled by the Taliban and their disrespect for art, beauty, books, and learning (aside from their narrow range of acceptable subjects): essentially everything celebrated by the region's poetry-infused heritage. Ironically, the word Taliban means "students," but their arrival forced half of Herat's students—all females—to cease their studies or go into hiding. This included Nadia Anjuman, who was in eleventh grade when the Taliban captured Herat in 1995, and had already been writing and reciting poems at home and school for years.

The remainder of this introduction concentrates on Nadia Anjuman's life and work rather than a broader survey of contemporary women poets for several reasons. First, Nadia's story has had a deeply significant impact on Herat's contemporary literary culture and psyche, particularly among the young women poets. Understanding her story, in many ways, is foundational

---

25   Christina Lamb, *Sewing Circles,* (Perennial, 2002) 160.

for understanding the context for other women writers since her death. Many of these poets have taken up activist causes, especially for women's rights, alongside their creative work, driven to protest the conditions that lead to deaths like Nadia's. Additionally, Nadia Anjuman was not only the first woman to publish a book of poems in Herat after the fall of Taliban, but was also widely considered one of the most promising young poets. It is appropriate, then, to dedicate the remainder of this introduction to her story and her memory.

As her older brother Mohammad Shafi Noorzayi told the story, Nadia's first impetus for writing poetry was her indignation at an injustice. She was in the fifth grade at Mahjūba Herawī School when she came home from class one day in tears. To her mother's inquiry, she replied, "It's not fair. My history teacher lowered my grade because I'm younger than the rest of the students, even though I answered all the questions correctly! And then he raised the grade of one of the lazy boys in the class—the one who is his nephew."[26]

Deeply disturbed by this unjust treatment, she stayed up that night filled with anxiety, and apparently poetic inspiration. The next day, Nadia went to school armed with the first poem she had ever written. It was about the corrupt grading incident, and she read it aloud in front of the headmaster. In addition to recognizing the young student's talent, the headmaster confronted her history teacher about his blatant corruption and favoritism. "This was all the motivation Nadia needed to write more poems," said Noorzayi. "From then on Nadia read her poetry at all of the school's ceremonies. Her classmates were proud of her, and her teachers were supportive and encouraging."[27]

Her family encouraged her too. Nadia was the sixth of eight children, several of whom were also artistically and poetically inclined. One of her close friends recalled Nadia telling the story about how

---

26   From a biographical note about Nadia written by M. Shafi Noorzayi, 23 Jan 2006, used courtesy of the author.

27   Noorzayi, 1.

her family would compose poems around the *dastarkhān* (table-cloth on the floor spread with food)—a sister would begin, a brother would say the next line, and so forth.[28] Her older sister Fawzia also wrote poems and became a Dari schoolteacher. Mohammad Shafi, who was just a year and a half older than Nadia, studied art and became an art teacher at the University. The extent of their support for her is evidenced by their permissiveness and encouragement during the Taliban years, when they allowed her to continue studying literature in secret, despite great risk. The women themselves initiated these meetings, and later several instructors joined the gatherings to guide and assist them. Laila Raziqi, one of Nadia's closest friends, described how they first began to meet and share their writing:

> We would gather in secret (hidden from the Taliban) with neighbors and former classmates. We did have actual sewing lessons in our home (my sister knew sewing), but studied other things too. This was before the group had a name. We would meet twice a week in our home. Nadia learned sewing very well. One day she came to me with a notebook (*chatalnawes*) and said, "I've written some poems but haven't shown them to anyone." She asked if I wanted to see, since I liked writing and such things. I saw that they were very good poems.[29]

Another member of the original group, Gulsoom Sediqi, remembers the great satisfaction the women got from these gatherings. When we met at her office at the Higher Education Institute where she now teaches law, she recounted, "For others it was laughable; what did four or five women want with literature in such a time? When even basic literacy and security were not available, what good would literature do? But it brought us joy."[30] Later, more women

---

28   Interview with Gulsoom Sediqi, 25 May 2013.

29   Interview with Laila Raziqi, 27 May 2013.

30   Interview with Gulsoom Sediqi, 25 May 2013.

joined them and they began meeting in the home of one of Nadia's neighbors, who happened to be the head of the Literature and Humanities Department at Herat University, Ustad Mohammad Naser Rahyab. Professor Rahyab had known Nadia since she was a little girl, as their families came from the same village of Ghuryun, close to the border with Iran. They remained neighbors in Herat, a distance of about 100 meters separating their front doors.

Grateful for a few minutes of his time, I sat in Professor (Ustad) Rahyab's busy office on the third floor of the peach-colored Humanities building on Herat University's campus as he recounted his many connections to Nadia: their family connections, common heritage, instructing her in his home during Taliban times, and later, being her professor at the University. He described her as hardworking, courteous, modest—and always having had the desire to write poems. "When you looked at her poems, you could see her taking steps toward finding her own voice and style, but she was young and had not arrived there yet," he recalled.[31]

It was during the time when the women were meeting at Ustad Rahyab's home that the course adopted the name *Sūzan-e Telāyī*, or "The Golden Needle," to throw the Taliban's scent off their illicit activities of reading and discussing Persian literature as well as foreign classics like Shakespeare and Tolstoy. The women would show up at Professor Rahyab's home with their sewing baskets, notebooks and pens hidden among the fabrics. Rahyab's wife played a vital role, poised to rapidly switch places with the literature professor in case the Taliban came to the door. Nadia began to share and refine her poems in the secret class setting, but she still did most of her writing at home. Her brother Shafi remembers her in the kitchen, her notebook never far away, composing as she cooked. She would write late into the night, when the house was still, after everyone else had gone to bed.

Another one of the professors who took the risk to instruct the determined women was Professor Mohammad Dawood Munir. He recalled some of Nadia's influences from those early days of

---

31   Interview with Ustad Rahyab, 26 May 2013.

her literary exploration. She loved classical Persian poets Hafez and Mowlana (Rumi)—and she admired Jami. She also read Nima Yushij (who is considered the father of modern Persian poetry) and Afghan poets including Qahar-e Aasi, Latif Nazemi, and Wasif Bakhtari. But she expressed a special devotion for Sohrab Sepehri. "How do I know she loved Sohrab's poems?" mused Dr. Munir. "Because in Taliban times when she would bring his poems to read, she would ask us relentlessly about their meaning; she wanted to really understand them." He also noted traces of Forugh Farrokhzad and Simin Behbahani in her poems. The instructors noticed Nadia's talents especially because she wrote in both classical and new styles, a skill that would later appeal to the broader literary community as well.

While Nadia had always been sensitive to injustice, during the Taliban years the excruciating situation of women in Afghanistan fueled her art all the more. One of her most famous poems, written in 1999, is called "Makes No Sense" (Abas).[32] Many know the poem by the name "Afghan Woman," or *Dokhte Afghan* after the song by Afghan musician Shahla Zaland setting Anjuman's poem to music. The first two couplets set a bleak scene:

نیست شوقی که زبان باز کنم از چه بخوانم
من که منفور زمانم چه بخوانم چه نخوانم

چه بگویم سخن از شهد که زهر است به کامم
وای از مشت ستمگر که بکوبیده دهانم

Music makes no sense anymore—when abandoned by time, who composes, whether singing or sitting still?

When words are poison to the tongue, why taste? Stifling songs is my abuser's strongest skill.[33]

---

32   Alternate translations of this title are "Useless" and "In Vain."

33   While a number of English translations exist for this poem, I humbly offer this one.

Despite the clearly pessimistic implication of the poem's title and first lines, Nadia's friends and teachers recall the persistent hopefulness in so many of her poems written during this time, a hopefulness which is evident even in "Makes No Sense." The poem continues,

من و این کنج اسارت، غم ناکامی و حسرت
که عبث زاده ام و مهر بباید به زبانم

دانم ای دل که بهار ان بود و موسم عشرت
من پربسته چه سازم که پریدن نتوانم

گرچه دیریست خموشم نرود نغمه ز یادم
ز انکه هر لحظه به نجوا سخن از دل بر هانم

...here, in this captive's cell with Grief and Remorse;
why live, if my tongue is sealed, still.

Slow down, heart that leaps to greet sweet spring,
my broken wings will temper this temporary thrill.

Though melodies drain from memory, stale with silence,
songs waft up from soul-whispers still.

When the situation seems hopeless, with the relentless questions, *why sing? why taste? why live?* echoing like a drumbeat of despair, she breaks in with the line "yet songs still waft up from soul-whispers." The "still-wafting" songs grow even stronger and louder at the end of the poem, with a defiant and even triumphant conclusion. The final lines are by far the most-remembered and oft-quoted lines of the poem, and Zaland's song:

یاد آن روز گرامی که قفس را بشکافم
سر برون آرم ازین عزلت و مستانه بخوانم

من نه آن بید ضعیفم که ز هر باد بلرزم
دخت افغانم و بر جاست که دایم به فغانم

One thought of the day I will break the cage
makes me croon like a carefree drunk until

they can see I am no wind-trembled willow tree—
an Afghan woman wails and sings, and wail and sing I will!

Despite the oppressive external realities during the Taliban times in Herat, Nadia's personal artistic life flourished. "It was in that secret class that she began to really grow as a poet," her brother Shafi recalled as we sat in his living room drinking tea and looking at pictures and videos of Nadia. Along with Professor Rahyab, professors Ahmad Sayeed Haqiqi and Dr. Mohammad Dawood Munir instructed the underground literature students in aesthetics, literary criticism, and poetic theory, helping them to refine their own short stories and poems. Dr. Munir remembered how the students called those moments the sweetest times of their lives—the heightened risk seemed to also heighten their appreciation of the precious knowledge they were receiving.[34]

Still, when the Taliban regime fell in 2001, it felt like a miraculous time of rebirth and opportunity.[35] Nadia and her companions from the *Sūzan-e Telāyī* group immediately set their sights on returning to their formal education. Mercifully, in December of that same year, Herat University opened up its entrance exam to women for the first time since they had been banished from the campus in 1995, adding a provision that those who had made it to eleventh grade before the Taliban could take the exam. Nadia Anjuman, along with Gulsoom Sediqi, Laila Raziqi, and four other women attempted that first exam, which would also determine their courses of study if they passed. Sediqi remembers how frigid it was during the exam, sitting in the *Bāgh-e Azādi* (Freedom Garden), and how the professors were rooting for them. Nadia, Gulsoom, and Laila, along with another poet named Naheed Baqi, were admitted

---

34 Interview with Ustad. Munir, 28 May 2013.

35 Almost everyone I spoke with in Herat described it this way, as a matter of fact or an obvious observation.

to Herat University's Literature Department to begin their course of study the following year.

Nadia Anjuman, still insatiable for learning, sped to the top of her class. Ustad Munir, who taught a class on poetic theory at that time, noted that the professors greatly respected her—most saw her as more of a colleague and an equal then merely a student.[36] Everyone expected her to join the university faculty upon graduation. Meanwhile, Nadia was continuing to hone her poetry through Literary Society meetings, newly reopened to women's participation. Herat's *Anjuman-e Adabī* had managed to sustain some operations during Taliban times, including the publication of its literary journal called *Aurang-e Hashtom,* or "The Eighth Throne," alluding to the Persian poet Jami's famous series of poems called *Haft Aurang,* or "Seven Thrones."

During Taliban times, as well as multiple earlier seasons of government pressure and censorship, the group had resolved to remain independent—refusing to publish government propaganda—or not remain open at all. In the early 2000s, after the Taliban's departure but in the face of renewed censorship from the self-proclaimed government of Ismail Khan,[37] the literary community nevertheless managed to launch a variety of new initiatives, including a youth branch called *Kānūn-e Jawānān-e Anjumane Adabī* in Dari. Nadia was an enthusiastic participant in this group, and also wrote for the section of the literary magazine dedicated to the youth, called *Aurang-e Jawānān,* or "The Throne of Youth."

Things changed drastically for Nadia when she got married. Nadia's confidants remember that she had no desire to marry, as she knew it would interfere with her education and artistic life. Instead, she had ambitions to pursue higher education all the way to the doctoral level. Gulsoom Sediqi told how their group of friends

---

36   Interview with Ustad Munir, 28 May 2013.

37   "All Our Hopes are Crushed: Violence and Repression in Western Afghanistan," Volume 14, Issue 7, Part 3. Human Rights Watch, January 1, 2002.

found out in their second year at Herat University that Nadia was getting married, and were shocked. "You would never have thought of Nadia as someone who would want to get married. She would want to be by herself," reflected Sediqi.[38] Nadia also thought marriage would be a barrier to her career and to her development as a writer.[39]

Many suitors had visited Nadia's family seeking her hand in earlier years, but she had made her wishes not to marry them clear and her family had respected those wishes, successfully deterring the suitors. Initially, the same was true for Farid Ahmad Majid Niā, a teaching assistant for a course in folklore (adabīyāt-e āmīyāna) that Nadia had taken. Laila Raziqi, who also took the folklore class, recalls that Farid "had a strange manner about him...nothing terribly wrong with him, but nothing really special." He was skinny and a poor student, whereas Nadia was among the best students, beautiful in mind and body. Majid Niā's family representatives first came asking for Nadia's hand (a process called khāstgāri in Dari) early in her course of study at the university. They received the same answer as the others: she was pursuing her education and not currently seeking to marry. However, they refused to give up. Some months would pass, and they would try again. This went on for two full years.

Finally, Majid Niā concocted a clever manipulation: he threatened to kill himself if Nadia did not consent to marry him, and sent his family members to Nadia's home bearing a Qur'an. Their message was along these lines: "We implore you, by all that's sacred, to give us Nadia, lest this lovesick young man lose his life because of her." This left Nadia and her family little choice. In part due to the social and religious pressures, and partly out of pity,[40] she reluctantly

---

38   Interview with Gulsoom Sediqi, 25 May 2013.

39   Biography of Nadia written by M. Shafi Noorzayi, Jan 23, 2006.

40   While we do not know for certain to what extent pity was a motivating factor, many of those close to her believed it to be a significant one, citing Nadia's compassionate nature.

agreed to the marriage. Their small, simple wedding ceremony took place during Nadia's third year at Herat University (2004). Majid Niā had no father, and his family was poor, uneducated, and very conservative.[41] The young man himself was educated in the same field as Nadia, however, and had a steady job, which gave her family hope that the match could work out. Yet Nadia's friends were not so sure. "This was not someone that Nadia could be with, and she knew it. She didn't want to marry him. Unfortunately, she was forced to do so," mourned Gulsoom Sediqi.[42]

According to the norm in Afghanistan, Nadia moved in with her husband's family, where much of the conflict ended up revolving around Nadia's new mother-in-law, to whom Majid Niā was very attached. Herself uneducated, Nadia's mother-in-law did not see Nadia's poetic ambitions and involvement with the literary community as particularly compatible with married life. The conflict intensified when Nadia became pregnant and gave birth to a baby boy, yet continued to attend classes and literary events, much to the displeasure of Majid Niā's mother. Ustad Rahyab described the situation this way:

> So when Nadia would say, "I'm off to the literary society," [her mother-in-law] would say "No. Better to take care of your kid so he won't cry." "No," Nadia would say, "I'm going." If this woman had been educated, she would not have objected. But as it was, she would say, "Why don't you wash the clothes?"[43]

Many also believe Majid Niā began getting jealous when Nadia's success outshone his own. It was her poems people loved, not his. Even the invitation cards for literary events would come in her name, not his.

After her marriage, the changes were not immediately apparent—at least on the surface. But Nadia began to go less frequently

---

41   Cited by Ustad Rahyab and others.

42   Interview with Gulsoom Sediqi, 25 May 2013.

43   Interview with Ustad Rahyab, 26 May, 2013.

to events at the Literary Society, and Laila Raziqi remembers that "her poems got darker."[44] Nadia was not one to complain and internalized most of her pain so few were aware of the extent of her problems at home. "She just put it all in her poems," said her friend Gulsoom Sediqi, who had switched to studying law, much to Nadia's consternation. While the friends saw less of each other, Sediqi wanted to do something about the state of women in Afghanistan, and thought the best way to do it was in the legal sphere.

In the meantime, Nadia had continued to hone her poetic skills, and Herat's Literary Society agreed to help her publish a book of her poems. The book bore the name of one of her most evocative pieces, *Gul-e Dūdi* ("Smoke-Bloom"), which begins,

من از احساس تهی بودن لبریزم
لبریز
و این فراوانی قحطی است که گهگاه مرا
در تب آتشیی مزرعه جانم
میجوشاند
و ازین جوشش بی آب عجیب
چهره کاغذی دفتر شعرم، ناگه
جان میگیرد

I'm full of the feeling of emptiness,
      full.
An abundant starvation
boils me in my soul's fevered fields,
and this strange waterless boiling
startles the image in my poem
      to life.[45]

---

44   Interview with Laila Raziqi, 27 May, 2013.

45   Author's translation.

When I asked Gulsoom Sediqi about the poem, she gave me the following poignant reflection on Nadia's meaning:

> When she was under pressure, she wrote…[saying] I wish I could go to a faraway place, but I can't, I don't have the feet to go. All I can do is write. And I feel that I am a wilted flower, without color—not red, a forgotten flower that is not seen. A unique flower, but stripped of color and scent.

> The "peerless rose" mentioned later in the poem *Gul-e Dūdī* is the image on the speaker's notebook (or alternately the images in her poems) which comes to life, but only lives briefly, before she is obscured by streaks and fumes of smoke. In the end, the metaphor in Nadia's poem is a heartbreakingly apt depiction of her own life.

Gul-e Dūdī was released in 2005, Nadia's fourth year of university, and the Literary Society held an event in honor of the book's publication. It was the first book of poems to be published by a female poet in Herat after the Taliban. Her family attended, along with a gathering of professors and students, and Gulsoom Sediqi served as the emcee for the event. It should have been a victorious moment. But "there was something over her, intimidating her, keeping her head down and voice low. Her husband was there too. One could feel the pressure that was on her." At the event, various noteworthy voices in the literary community spoke about Nadia's poems, and Sediqi noticed Majid Niã's growing displeasure at all the attention she was getting. Ustad Munir remembered reading several of her poems at that event, and telling the gathering that Nadia was shouting her own pain and the pain of her whole society in her poems. "She screamed it. Her cry was in her poems but we did not pay attention… We only had this knowledge in the language of poetry." Somaia Ramish, one of the younger poets, heard Nadia reading her poems and "wanted very much to be like her, to be accepted like her."[46]

---

46   Interview with Somaia Ramish, 28 May 2013.

Gulsoom Sediqi recalled the last time she saw Nadia, at a literary event to critique another person's poems. It was a brisk late-October day, and Nadia wore black clothes and a black scarf (chador) as she often did. Her husband was with her. Nadia had prepared an analysis of the poetry, and they invited her up to speak. "She went up to the stage to read it, and did not raise her head even once," said Sediqi, describing how there were mostly men in the room and mentioning again the husband's presence. "When Nadia went back to sit down, she saw me, took my hand, kissed my face very earnestly and said 'I've missed you so much.' We talked very warmly together. It was exactly ten days later that she died."

Ten days after Gulsoom and Nadia saw each other, it was Eid-e Fitr, the holiday observed at the conclusion of the month of Ramadan. On the evening of November 5th, 2005, Nadia and her husband had an argument at home about the holiday visits, and the altercation turned violent. Neighbors later testified that they heard yelling and what sounded like a violent fight. Nadia was taken to the hospital four hours after she died, and the medical report cited bruising around the ear and other evidence of hard blows (perhaps by a TV remote or cell phone) to the side of her head. The report stated that the cause of death was bleeding in the brain. Others also witnessed the bruising. That night, Majid Niā admitted to slapping her, but not killing her, claiming that she later committed suicide by taking poison. Her death sent shockwaves through Herat, the rest of Afghanistan, and even made the news in the U.K., the U.S., and elsewhere.[47]

The days and weeks that followed were saturated with memorial events and poetry readings in honor of Nadia Anjuman, including dozens of poems written in her honor (*mersiyeh*, poems written at the death of a loved one). "When Nadia died, the entire city was affected," recalled her brother Shafi. "Everyone wept,

---

47 See "Afghan Poet Dies after battering." *BBC News.* 6 Nov 2005, and "Afghan Poet Dies After Beating by Husband," by Carlotta Gall, *New York Times.* 8 Nov 2005.

everyone prayed, people made films, songs, and poems. Not only in Herat, but in Kabul, Mazar, and outside of Afghanistan too, like in Germany. We even got a message from the president and some of the ministers came to our house. The whole intellectual community of Herat came to us to express their sorrow and regret, and to condemn the killer. All the media covered it." Majid Niā and his mother were both initially arrested, but only Nadia's husband remained in jail awaiting prosecution. There was a national and international outpouring of support from human rights and women's rights organizations for Nadia's case, to see that justice was done. An attorney and judge were even brought in from Kabul so that they could work independently and not be corrupted. Activists wanted to see the case become an example showing that men could not simply get away with crimes of domestic violence. Simultaneously, the elders of Majid Niā's family visited Anjuman's family on multiple occasions to intercede on his behalf (was it eerily reminiscent of when they had come entreating Nadia's family for her hand in marriage?). They asked the family to forgive him, saying it had been an accident, a mistake. After the fifth or sixth such visit, they brought a Qur'an with them to add weight to their plea.

In the end, Nadia's family decided that forgiveness was greater in God's eyes than revenge, and also believed it to be in the interest of Nadia's young son, Bahram Sayeed, to have mercy on his father. Nadia's brother Shafi explained that they also were not interested in an involved court case that kept the open wound of Nadia's death festering for even longer, and they did not want Nadia to become an object to be used for political purposes. They wanted to begin to try to forget, and heal. One of the assurances they received from legal counsel in the midst of this process, however, was that even if they pardoned him, Majid Niā would be in prison for five years. The evidence from the medical report and other witnesses was enough to convict Majid Niā, but the pardon would lighten his punishment. In the end, the family decided five years of incarceration would be sufficient. They also decided not to take custody of the infant Bahram, since by law custody would revert to the father when he reached seven years of age, and they considered it far more difficult to say goodbye to a seven-year-old than a six-month-old.

Around four months later, however, Majid Niā was free (apparently through a corrupt deal), and Anjuman's family had been cheated out of even a small measure of justice. Despite this additional bitter blow, Nadia's family could take comfort in the honored place of respect and fond remembrance that the people of Herat, and especially the literary community, hold for the poet whom some called "Afghanistan's Lady of Ghazals" *(Banū-e Ghazal-e Afghanistan)*. "Not one of us, her professors or colleagues at the Literary Society, can ever forget her, she whose very surname was *Anjuman*. She herself chose that name. The choice of this name, too, returns to her motivation to write and love for the literary society, and for literature and culture," affirmed Ustad Munir.

The acknowledgment of Nadia's life and poetic contributions is important to the current endeavor for several reasons. Nadia was the first and, by all accounts, the best female poet in Herat's literary community in the early post-Taliban years. In many ways she set the bar high for other female poets, and has undoubtedly has inspired many. Her poems expressed personal experience and imagination, but also connected profoundly with the experience of the majority of Afghan women. "In her poems," Ustad Munir reflected, "Nadia Anjuman simultaneously expressed her own personal voice, as well as speaking the unspoken laments of the other women of her society." Using Nadia's own metaphor, the professor summarized the tragedy of Nadia's loss: "In post-Taliban years, Nadia was an important poet who bloomed, and who wilted far too quickly."[48]

Yet Somaia Ramish was quick to remind me that Nadia's story is hardly unique, and not merely an isolated incident of domestic violence. Nadia's situation was one of many examples of broader societal patterns of gendered violence, double standards for men and women, and impunity for (male) criminals. "Her death was

---

48   Interview with Ustad Munir, 28 May 2013.

horrible, unthinkable for all of us," Somaia told me. "But physical death is not the only kind of death. One kind of death is physical— of the body, another kind of death is spiritual—of the heart. And that is a worse death."[49]

She implied that countless women, women who perhaps could be great poets (but who will ever know?), experience this death of the heart and are forgotten far sooner than Nadia ever will be. "In the ten years I've been at the Literary Society, so many women have come and gone, and they are lost, hidden. Maybe they publish something, maybe not. No one asks after them. Only when some- one is killed or sets themselves on fire, they make a symbol out of them. Why don't they ask, where is such-and-such? Or, where is so-and-so [while they are *alive*]?" The real tragedy, she said, was the norm that allowed women to be forgotten before they had even died physically, and never discover the poet (or artist, or engineer, or business leader) they could have been. Her observations brought into relief the achievement represented by the women who have persevered to write, and get their work published.

If the *Anjuman-e Adabī* offered Nadia the soil of a community in which to grow, many other emerging poets continue to respond to that opportunity. On the afternoon I visited Herat's gathering of poets, there were around fifteen to eighteen young men present, and six or seven women. A few participants came and went in the course of the two and a half hours of the gathering. It struck me that almost everyone in the group was very young, most of them in their twenties, and even one fellow who looked to be about 15. This was the place where young Herati writers cut their teeth, working to produce new pieces worthy of the weekly gauntlet of lively criti- cism from peers and more experienced poets, such as the modera- tor. If a poet improved to the point where the society felt his or her work deserved a broader audience, then they might publish a collection of the poet's work, with their imprint, as they did with Nadia.

---

49   Interview with Somaia Ramish, 28 May 2013.

Several of the poets featured in this collection were present at the literary society gatherings I attended in 2013 and 2014 and are active in the literary community. I have endeavored to include poets whose work has been recognized and anthologized in Persian-language publications in Afghanistan. All of them have published at least one collection of poetry, or have a publication forthcoming. Their work also appears in one or more anthologies of Herati, Afghan or international poets published since 2001, five of which I have consulted in the making of this book.

GENERAL NOTE ON THE TRANSLATIONS

IMPERFECTION MAY BE the most dependable trait of any translated poem. But is it possible that these imperfections, these bumps and dents where text or subtext, tone or undertone fail to match precisely, if they are handled with care on the poet's wheel, could make the translation a more pleasing, more authentic vessel? Like the potter's bowl, a poem translation exists to convey, to carry ideas and images from one language to another. The vessel should not be jagged or awkward, should not distract from the taste of the meanings within. A quality container, on the other hand, though humble, can enhance the savoring of the substance. Its "flaws" do not have to detract from that experience, as the translated poem should complement, should honor, should bear the original to new readers, new connoisseurs, but is not pretending to *be* that original.

This is not to say that a translation, that *these* translations, could not be better. In fact, I am certain they could. I would hope that (as with any art) greater experience and intimacy with the context, the language, the poets themselves, would yield better translations, better vessels. There are also many voices missing from this small collection, work by worthy poets that I have had to omit, and I can only hope to make up for these shortfalls by continuing to translate.

Rather than an extended reflection on the translations here, I have introduced each of the poets with a brief biography and a section specifically addressing the translation of her poems. This decision reflects the unique experience (should I say struggle? adventure?) of translating the work of each poet. It also serves as a gesture toward the deeper literary analysis that this work deserves.

With that in mind, a few general observations suffice to set the stage for the reading of the translations as a whole. For each poem, the Dari text appears on the right, while the English is on the left. For multi-page poems, the page breaks follow a rough, although not exact, correspondence. Many of the Dari poems do not have titles, and I have supplied English ones for the sake of reference and delineating which poem is which. Where the Dari poem was designated simply as a "ghazal," I kept that convention, numbering them for clarity. In addition, the reader will notice that some poems include a date at the bottom while others do not; this is simply based on whether or not the poet provided one in the original text. Here I have chosen to use the year only, for consistency, although some gave specific months as well.

I have made minor punctuation and spelling edits to the Dari versions of the poems. Where the edits were slightly more substantive, such as a word changed or letter added to tighten the meter, the poet's approval was sought whenever possible. Otherwise, I have reproduced the poems as they appeared in the poets' books or as they were sent to me by electronic means.

The book's title, *Load Poems Like Guns,* comes from a poem by Somaia Ramish, reminiscent of Emily Dickinson's poem no. 754, which begins, "My Life has stood—a Loaded Gun—" While the specific intentions behind Dickinson's and Ramish's poems are different, the general intent is similar: to invoke the violent image of a weapon, commonly associated with men, and appropriate it (either its actual voice or its use) as a means of inverting expectations. In Dickinson's poem no. 754, the speaker's life takes on the form of everything contrary to what her culture expected of ideal female (soft, nurturing, pleasant, weak), presenting itself as hard, emphatic, even cruel and violent.[50]

---

50   Paula Bennett, *My Life a Loaded Gun: Female Creativity and Feminist Poetics.* (Beacon Press, 1986) 6.

Ramish uses an urgent, imperative tone:

> Load your poems—
> your body—
> your thoughts—
> like guns.

"War's geography," she says, calls for an equally aggressive response. She urges that verses be filled with ammunition as if to say: *no softness or compliance here, this is not the time for love-songs.* Like Dickinson's poem, this one implies an imminent "unladylike" explosion. Ramish's poem captures the "fighting" spirit evident in much of the work of Herat's contemporary women poets, for whom poetry is a means of actively participating in the intellectual and socio-political struggles of their time.

NADIA ANJUMAN

نادیا انجمن

(1980-2005)

Born on December 27th, 1980, Nadia Anjuman (Nādiā Anjuman) grew up in a home that encouraged her writing and a small literary community that nurtured her skills, even during Taliban times. She was among the first women to take the entrance exam and enroll in Herat University after the fall of the Taliban, but her pursuit of a degree in Literature was cut short when she was killed by her husband on November 4th, 2005, just short of her 25th birthday. Her chosen pen name honors her beloved Herat Literary Society, or *Anjuman-e Adabīye Herat*.

Nadia Anjuman. Photo courtesy of Mohammad Shafi Noorzayi.
Book cover of *Gul-e Dūdī* by Nadia Anjuman, used by permission.

Note on the Translations

Nadia wrote many of her poems in traditional Persian forms such as the *ghazal*, a poem made up of five to fifteen grammatically independent couplets, utilizing a refrain and rhyming pattern directly preceding the refrain. In Persian (as well as other languages like Arabic, Urdu, and Turkish) the form adheres to a strict metrical pattern and usually addresses themes like love, longing, and existential questions. Herat's literary community considered her one of the most skilled young poets of her generation with regard to classical forms like the *ghazal*. One of the challenges of translating formal verse such as Nadia's is how to preserve or recreate these forms in the English language...or whether to attempt to do so at all. Does a formal approach to translation facilitate the reader's access to the sounds and rhythms of the original piece, or does it run the risk of polluting meaning by attempting to fit ideas into forms that work very differently in the destination language?

From Nadia's collection, I've selected several formal poems, including one of her most well-known works, *Abas* ("Makes No Sense"). Many Afghans know this poem by the name *Dūkht-e Afghān* ("Afghan Girl"), a song by musician Shahla Zaland that uses Nadia's poem as lyrics. Among the three formal poems in this selection, *Abas* is the only poem I have aligned loosely to the ghazal-form in English. For Nadia's other ghazals, *Bāgh-e Man* ("My Garden") and *Husn-e Khudāyī* ("Divine Beauty"), I found it more effective to capture an echo of the rhythm through internal and slant-rhymes. All of the poems included here are found in her collection, *Smoke-Bloom* (2005).

MAKES NO SENSE

Music makes no sense anymore—why should I compose,
I am abandoned by time whether I sing or am still.

When words are poison to the tongue, why taste?
Stifling songs is my abuser's strongest skill.

No one anywhere notices or cares whether
I cry, whether I laugh, whether I die or am still

here, in this captive's cell with Grief and Remorse;
why live, if my tongue is sealed, still.

Slow down, heart that leaps to greet sweet spring,
my broken wings will temper this temporary thrill.

Though melodies drain from memory, stale with silence,
songs waft up from soul-whispers still.

One thought of the day I will break the cage
makes me croon like a carefree drunk until

they can see I am no wind-trembled willow tree—
an Afghan woman wails and sings, and wail and sing I will!

(1999)

عبث

نیست شوقی که زبان باز کنم از چه بخوانم
من که منفور زمانم چه بخوانم چه نخوانم

چه بگویم سخن از شهد که زهر است به کامم
وای از مشت ستمگر که بکوبیده دهانم

نیست غمخوار مرا در همه دنیا به که نازم
چه بگویم، چه بخندم، چه بمیرم، چه بمانم

من و این کنج اسارت، غم ناکامی و حسرت
که عبث زاده ام و مهر بباید به زبانم

دانم ای دل که بهار ان بود و موسم عشرت
من پربسته چه سازم که پریدن نتوانم

گرچه دیریست خموشم نرود نغمه ز یادم
ز انکه هر لحظه به نجوا سخن از دل بر هانم

یاد آن روز گرامی که قفس را بشکافم
سر برون آرم ازین عزلت و مستانه بخوانم

من نه آن بید ضعیفم که ز هر باد بلرزم
دخت افغانم و بر جاست که دایم به فغانم

۱۳۷۸

MOUNTAIN, SEA

Oh, exiles of Mount Namelessness,
your jeweled names asleep beneath mute swamplands,
your effaced memories, light blue memories!
Where amid murky brainwaves in this sea of forgetfulness
does the clear current of your thoughts run?

Which plunderer's hand has stolen your golden-sculpted dreams?
Any trace of your serene moon-silver boat in this despotic storm?
Any trace of life in this cold-fingered morgue?

If the sea fell still,
if the clouds emptied the heart's heaviness;
if the moon-lady smiled
her affection,

if the mountain's heart softened,
                    turned fertile,
would one of your names ascend
to the heights of sunlight?

Will any hope-traces catch the light in your memories,
your light blue memories, as they rise
in the frightened eyes of tired fish
barraged by black floodrains?

Oh, exiles of Mount Namelessness!

(2001)

کوه، دریا

ایا تبعیدیان کوه گمنامی
ای گوهران نامهاتان خفته در مرداب خاموشی
ای محو گشته یادهاتان،
یادهای آبی روشن
به ذهن موج گل آلود دریای فراموشی

زلال جاری اندیشه هاتان کو؟
کدامین دست غارتگر به یغما برد
تندیس طلای ناب رویاتان

درین طوفان ظلمتزا
کجا شد زورق سیمین آرامش نشان ماه پیماتان

پس از این زمهریر مرگزا
دریا اگر آرام گیرد
ابر اگر خالی کند از عقده ها دل
دختر مهتاب اگر مهر آورد،
لبخند بخشد

کوه اگر دل نرم سازد، سبزه آرد
بارور گردد
یکی از نامهاتان، بر فراز قله ها
خورشید خواهد شد؟

طلوع یادهاتان
یادهای آبی روشن
به چشم ماهیان خسته از سیلاب و
از باران ظلمت ها هراسان
جلوه امید خواهد شد؟
ایا تبعید یان کوه گمنامی!

۱۳۸۳

My Garden

I'd like to grasp the word *hope,* and with it barricade
sorrow's path as I devise another road.

Life's vines demand irrigation, but I
want to drink tomorrow's worries like wine.

I'd like to flush even shadows from moon's fountain;
to paint cypress trees and meadows fortune-green.

If I invite the sun to this scene, the light will reveal
that my garden is the envy of jewels.

Time will write the tale of my life's toil;
but I'd like to fill history's chest with gold.

If my voice could be celebrated, my songs nursed,
I'd gild every notebook with elegant verse.

(2000)

باغ من

دوست دارم معنی امید را باور کنم
راه غم بر بندم و فکر ره دیگر کنم

رشته های زندگی را آبیاری لازم است
بعد ازین آینده را نوشاب در ساغر کنم

چشمه مهتاب را در سایه ها جاری کنم
سرو ها و سبزه ها را سبز در اختر کنم

باغ من در روشنی رشک گوهرمیشود
گر گل خورشید را دعوت به این محشر کنم

روزگار از کار من افسانه ای خواهد نوشت
دوست دارم سینه تاریخ را پر زر کنم

انجمن گر در سرودنها مرا یاری کند
شعر ناب خویش را آزین هر دفتر کنم

۱۳۷۹

DIVINE BEAUTY

At every turn I saw your features etched in the dawn,
heard tales of you from Shahrazad's tongue.

You wrote the tune to every poem I composed
while every word I pondered took your shape.

I sense no sorrow in breaking away from society—
I took the lonely path to follow you.

To my chilled midnight you're the golden chandelier,
to my branches you're the dream of hundred-hued blooms.

You, forest's fragrant draw, spring's waking breath—
you, illumined muse to my dim page; you, fateful smile!

Even among world champions of grace and charm,
amid beauty ineffable and divine, you're the first of your kind.

(2002)

حسن خدایی

به هر کجا که رسیدم طلوع روی تو دیدم
ز شهرزاد خوش آوا، حکایت تو شنیدم

به هرچه شعر سرودم ترانه ساز تو بودی
خیال نقش تو بود آنچه روی صفحه کشیدم

اگر ز خلق گسستم چه غم که با تو نشستم
اطاعت تو گزیدم اگر ز جمع بریدم

به ظلمت شب سردم تو چلچراغ طلایی
طراوت گل صدرنگ شاخه های امیدم

شمیم دلکش جنگل، نسیم صبح بهاری
تو جلوهٔ شب شعرم، تو لطف بخت سپیدم

به بزم ماه لقایان، میان مجلس خوبان
به کبریایی حسن خدایی تو ندیدم

۱۳۸۱

45

SMOKE-BLOOM

I'm full of the feeling of emptiness,
full.
An abundant famine
boils me in my soul's fevered fields,
and this strange waterless boiling
startles the image in my poem
to life.
I watch the new-living picture,
a peerless rose
blush across the page!

But barely has she first breathed,
when streaks of smoke begin
to obscure her face and fumes
consume her perfumed skin.

(2002)

گل دودی

من از احساس تهی بودن لبریزم
لبریز
و این فراوانی قحطی است که گهگاه مرا
در تب آتشیی مزرعه جانم
میجوشاند
و ازین جوشش بی آب عجیب
چهره کاغذی دفتر شعرم، ناگه
جان میگیرد

گل میاندازد
گل بیمانندی است
ولی افسوس تنش را
رگه هایی از دود
رنگ و بو میبخشد

۱۳۸۱

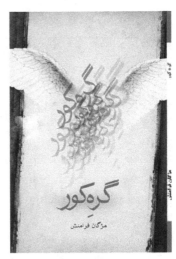

MUZHGAN FARAMANESH

مژگان فرامنش

(1990-)

Muzhgan Faramanesh (Muzhgān Farāmanesh) was born in 1990 in the city of Herat, where she has lived her whole life. She is completing her final year at Herat University, with a degree in Persian Language and Literature. She is also an active member of the Herat Literary Society, where she participates in the weekly poetry workshops. Her first collection of poems, titled *Andīshahāy-e dard-ālud* (*Pain-Tainted Reflections*) was published in 2011 in Herat. Her second collection, *Gereye Kūr (Blind Knot)*, is forthcoming. Her work has been featured in numerous journals such as *Aurang-e Hashtom (The Eighth Throne),* a publication of Herat Literary Society), radio and TV programs, and anthologies including, *Īnjā naguftahā ast (There is Much Left Unsaid Here),* published by Herat Literary Society's Youth Club in 2010.

Muzhgan Faramanesh. Photo courtesy of Muzhgan Faramanesh.
Book cover of *Gereye Kūr,* courtesy of Muzhgan Faramanesh.

Note on the Translations

Muzhgan Faramanesh writes primarily in formal verse, including classical forms such as the *ghazal, rubāyī* (quatrain), and *masnawī* (rhyming couplets). While the Persian language, with its usual placement of verbs at the end of the thought or sentence, lends itself to metered verse with repeated end-words (mono-rhymes), other languages tend to be more stubborn to coax into this form. Contemporary Persian language poets including Faramanesh, are playing with these classical forms, not only introducing modern objects and topics—like cigarettes and suicide bombs—but also breaking with the tight conventions of the form. Many modern ghazal-writers, for instance, have disposed with the requirement of invoking their own name in the final couplet of a ghazal. It is appropriate, then, that translations of these ghazals should also seek to be reminiscent of the form while not being too tightly constrained by it—a somewhat precarious balancing act.

Translations also grapple with implied meanings: how to remain subtle while employing a tone or a phrase that suggests an idea conveyed indirectly or intuitively in the original. For example, I have translated the final verse of the second ghazal included in Faramanesh's selection this way:

من پر از ذره های باروت و درتنم آتشی فروزان است
خود کشی، مرگ، زندگی، یا عشق؟ طعمه ی گرم انتحار شوم.

I am strewn with gunshot residue; my body aglow in fire:
self-kill, live, love, or die? I'll be the warm prey of someone's suicide.

In the original Persian Dari, Faramanesh uses two words for suicide: *khud-kushī* and *entehār.* The former is closer to what I have translated as "self-kill," while the latter is often associated with suicide bombing (*enfejār-e entehari*). The poet does not used any words related to bombing, but the idea of being a victim, being the "warm prey" of this kind of suicide, as well as the common usage of *entehār,* makes a compelling case for implying the same in English. Rather than add a more obvious word like "bomb" or "explosion," I chose to use the phrase "someone's suicide," hinting that there is another person involved—this death by suicide is not at the speaker's own hands.

This final verse also represents a twist on the traditional ghazal theme: love and/or the unattainable beloved. The poem initially seems to align closely to this formality, but ultimately disrupts it at the end by suggesting that the speaker herself may be the unattainable beloved, due to the violence she endures.

The two ghazals represent two different approaches to translating this type of form. The first one remains relatively close to the rules, with the initial verse rhyming both halves (both lines of the "couplet") and retaining that rhyme for each *beit* (verse in two lines). I used end rhymes—pain/veins/terrain/stain/sustained, with pain repeated twice—an appropriate emphasis for the theme of the poem. The second ghazal, however, did not lend itself to such close formal adherence. Instead, I chose a series of slant and internal rhymes within each *beit*, offering a sense of rhythm while seeking to avoid stiltedness.

Ghazal 1

May God keep you from even a moment of sorrow and pain
May he pour long from love's ample cup into your life's veins.

May he keep your eyes from drowning in dew
though God knows mine have seen their share of pain.

May he take you to the lovely garden of songs,
Keep drought far from your heart's terrain.

May you not be like me, craving to write the ferocity of grief
but deprived of the ink to record its stain.

Even though I'm weary and wracked with desire,
May God spare you the suffering I've sustained.

غزل

خدا برای تو یک لحظه درد و غم ندهد
به زندگی تو از جام عشق کم ندهد.

اگرچه درد زیادی برای من داده است
ولی برای تو چشمی که غرق نم...ندهد.

تو را به باغ قشنگ ترانه ها ببرد
به سرزمین دلت خشکسالی هم ندهد.

به مثل من نشوی تا که از سر اندوه
بخواهی و به نویسی ولی قلم ندهد.

اگرچه خسته ام وسخت آرزو دارم
خدا برای تو دردی که میکشم ندهد.

Ghazal 2

Like crack-prone glass, like a mirror's dusty haze—
God fashioned me restless for your love's gaze.

Be for me breath, be for me just the reason for being—
when you forsake me, I take on the load of endless ache.

I am strewn with fall's footprints and winter's bitter tale—
where will spring arrive with this body's branches dry?

Days play out on a somber stage, I brim with unsure hope,
I drown in disarray—without you when will I be whole?

I am strewn with gunshot residue; my body aglow in fire:
self-kill, live, love, or die? I'll be the warm
prey of someone's suicide.

غزل

و خدا آفرید تا اینکه من از عشق تو بیقرار شوم
مثل آیینه ها شکستنی و مثل آیینه پرغبار شوم.

تو برایم فقط نفس باشی تو برایم دلیل بودن ها
تو به یکباره بگذری ازمن، صاحب درد بیشمار شوم.

من پر از رد پای پاییز وقصه ی تلخ یک زمستانم
در تنم شاخه ها خشکیده ست، من کجا میشود بهار شوم؟

روزها صحنه های غمگین اند، من پر از انتظار نامعلوم
قلب من غرق درد وآشوب است من بدون تو کی تیار شوم؟

من پر از ذره های باروت و درتنم آتشی فروزان است
خود کشی، مرگ، زندگی، یا عشق؟ طعمه ی گرم انتحار شوم.

Quatrain 1

I've grown used to black headscarves
I've grown used to moon-starved nights.

I've grown used to always singing
pain-soaked ghazals from inside the well.

با روسری سیاه عادت کردم
شب های بدون ماه عادت کردم.

با گریه ی واژه های پر درد غزل
هر لحظه درون چاه عادت کردم.

Quatrain 2

I am mirror and dust runs through me—
endless expectation runs through me.

I am the most wingless bird in history—
boundless loneliness runs through me.

آیینه ام و غبار درمن جاریست.
دنیای از انتظار در من جاریست.

بی بال ترین پرنده ی تاریخم.
دلتنگی بیشمار درمن جاریست.

QUATRAIN 3

You make my inner poems rhyme,
beauty of my fate's toppled bowl—

This poem may be colder than cold,
but you stoke the heat of my crazed soul.

تو قافیه شعر درونم هستی.
زیبایی بخت سر نگونم هستی

این شعر اگرچه سرد سرد است ولی.
گرمای دل پراز جنونم هستی.

QUATRAIN 4

After you, the song will lose its voice,
the mirror will be parted from the sky.

After you, oh lord of love, I can see
there will be an uproar in the city.

بعد از تو ترانه بی صدا خواهد شد.
آیینه از آسمان جدا خواهد شد

بعد از تو خدای عشق! باور دارم.
درشهر قیامتی به پا خواهد شد.

FARIBA HAIDARI

فریبا حیدری

(1980-)

Fariba Haidari (Farībā Haīdarī) was born in 1980 and holds a bachelor's degree. Her poetry collection, *Wa āwāz-hāye benafshe beqānūn* (*And Violet Tunes of Lawlessness*), was published in Herat in 2007. Her work also appears in collections including *Haq bā tamāme durūgh-hā ast* (*Lies Have the Right of Way*, 2005), a large anthology of Herati poets, both male and female, called *Kojāhā hanūz estāda-and* (*Where Do They Now Stand?* 2008), and two anthologies by Herat Literary Society's Youth Club: *Īnjā chahārshanbe ast* (*It is Wednesday Here*) and *Īnjā naguftahā ast* (*There is Much Left Unsaid Here*), both published in 2010. While Haidari's poetry included in this collection was written and published in Herat post-2001, she now lives in Sweden. She has two additional manuscripts of poetry ready for publication.

Fariba Haidari. Photo courtesy of Fariba Haidari.

Book cover of *Wa āwāz-hāye benafshe beqānūn* by Fariba Haidari. Photo by Farzana Marie

Note on the Translations

In the foreword to Fariba Haidari's collection of poems, Professor Mohammad Dawood Munir writes, "You can't just read Haidari's poems once. You have to read them over and over, sleep on them, become close friends with them."[1] I found this to be true. Haidari's poems are the longest individual pieces included in this volume. They can also be the most difficult to follow, frequently beginning in medias res, mid-thought, or mid-image. Even the title of the poet's collection begins with the word *wa* (and), as if in the middle of a sentence. Dreams and dream-language make frequent appearances, blurring the lines between reality and imagination and giving the poems a kind of floating, surreal quality, often jumping between abstract scenes or expressionist images.

To make these poems as readable as possible in translation while hopefully preserving these unique characteristics, I took some liberties in crafting the English versions. In several places I removed lines that did not, in my opinion, add to the experience of the poem. Some of these lines were repetitions that seemed less powerful (or, conversely, overly melodramatic) in English. Others were phrases like "I think / I suppose" which was implied by the lines that followed and did not enhance the poem's flow, sound, or meaning in English.

Despite their inclination toward surrealism, Fariba's poems are grounded in a variety of concrete and often repeated imagery such as stars, rain, wind, and the color violet (which she associates with death), which accumulate to form a pile of multi-layered meaning. A clear emphasis on the senses, especially smell, also permeates Haidari's poetry. Journeys or threads of related sensual imagery often provide the glue for entire poems, as in "Odor of Death," where smells of colors, of gunpowder in the garden, and repeated encounters with the odor of death punctuate the poem.

---

1   Foreword, *Wa āwāz-hāye benafshe beqānūn* (2005)

"And Violet Tunes of Lawlessness," the title poem for Haidari's collection, is a halting, rather unruly lyric on memory and legacy, or the residue of one's life. Creating an intentionally muddled speaker, the poet explores the consciousness of an artist longing to preserve history yet unable remember it, perhaps because of trauma, loss, and the lack of a suitable companion to remind her even of her own existence. The speaker, it seems, is in search of "A simple, distant secret, / familiar with the breath of skin...", one that will make space in her poems "for all the suns ever set." The poem, addressed to the absent companion, repeatedly echoes the question, *Why can't I remember? Why can't I recall?*

The speaker's search for evidence of her own existence, her identity, and the mark her life will leave is related to tracking down the history of loss. "Can you recall where / I lost you / or where / in the dirt my fingerprints / were?" Not receiving an answer, the speaker (whose concerns seem to correlate closely with those of the poet), ends the poem by positing that there may in fact be no trace of her (she may not even have existed): "or perhaps those weren't prints, just / a remnant / of the moon's shadow." While apparently self-deprecating, the irony is that the very lines on the *printed* page refute this logic. The poet, and by extension, the speaker she has created, *did* leave a mark.

ODOR OF DEATH

Odor of death
odor of orange and yellow roses
          like the shout that stuck in your throat
amplified with silence

and everyone knows the black clock of morning
struck several times with hands
that smell of rust

and the sun,
          having acquired the art of blindness,
          hauls its suffocation toward nightfall,
impregnates your evenings
born beyond the dreams
                    of gods.

What an impossible load!
Miracles newly decomposing,
as the smell of gunpowder permeates
          the flower beds

before the cocks start crowing,
your seed is spread

for the fourth time
they have taken your melodies
where snow-silvered mountains mock
          my amorphous borders
and the sun
                    once again prepares condolences
                    for its dead newborns.

بوی مرگ

بوی رُزهای نارنجی و زرد
مثل فریادی که نکرده ای
و بلند تر است

و همه می دانند
ساعت سیاه صبح
چند بار زنگ زده است
با عقربه هایی
که بوی اکسید آهن میدهد

و خورشید
با کوری اکتسابی اش
خفگی خودش را تا غروب حمل می کند
و آبستن می کند
شب هایت را
که بیرون از خواب خدایان
شکل گرفته اند

چه حمل ناممکنی!
جنازهٔ معجزه های تازه
که بوی باروت و باغچه می دهد

تو تکثیر می شوی
پیش از آنکه خروس ها به گریه بیفتند

برای بار چهارم
آواز هایت را برده اند
تا کوه های نقره ای دور
بی شکلی مرز ها مرا مسخر کنند
و آفتاب
بر نوزادان مرده اش
تسلیتی دوباره طرح بزند

Where are you taking my long dresses?

Behind this stream without source
        where I misplaced my diaphragm
                I had a nightmare wrapped in violet ribbons,
woke sweating cold

and your breath came heavy
        from a bruised larynx

and my hands follow the long violet trail
until they are entangled with you.

Where are you taking me
with my long dresses
carrying now the odor of the dead?

And time has passed
by the funeral procession of my thoughts
and the one who blew the trumpet
announcing death
        wished for the scent of windows
before last night.

I doubted the goodness of God and sometimes
I doubt the devil

I take pity on myself, bound
by shackles that took out a loan
on the fragrance of heaven

relying on roosters that lie sleeping
precisely as long as the night.

کجا می بری پیراهن های بلند؟

پشت این جریان بی مبدا
که گم شده بود عضله های تنفسی ام،
داشتم کابوس روبان های بنفش را
عرق می کردم

و تنفس تو
از حنجره ای که کبود

و دنبالهٔ این بنفش های طولانی
دست هایم به تو گره میخورد

به کجا می بری مرا؟
با پیراهن های بلند
که بوی کافور می دهد هنوز؟

اندی قرن از تشییع فکر هایم گذشته است
کسی که در صور می دمید
به گمانم
بوی پنجره های قبل از دیشب را
آرزو می کرد

تو را آورد
و مرا
فقط از تکه های تردیدیم
به خنده های خوب خدا هم
شک میکنم گاهی
به ابلیس

با دلسوزی مدام خودم برای خودم

و زنجیرها
که بوی بهشت را به عاریت گرفته اند
و خروس ها که می خوابند
درست به وقت مردن شب

I fall asleep.
In my dream I add
black mornings to my days.
All of me is learning to follow you,
    long skirts billowing around you,
graceful hands reaching
for infinity.

Tell me what lie
loosed your curls wild,
set the folds of your chador aflame
in the rain?

The one who wrapped the corpse of my youth in a grave—
shroud
looked like me
with a shout that got stuck in my throat
                amplified with silence.

Now I protest more against my bones
and the ashes of cold decomposed epics
and blood that hides
    from seasonal rains

and I am afraid
of the one who comes
to gather pieces of you
from this road, lying
that they had set you on fire
                again
in the moths' dreams.

(2005)

من خوابم می بود
من در خواب /
صبح های سیاه را به عمرم اضافه می کنم
من یاد می گیرم
با همهٔ قطره های تنم
دنبال تو راه بروم
و پیراهن های بلند را
در تو برقصانم

با دست هایی
که به خورشید های بی مبدأ
اشاره می کنند

بگو کدام دروغ
گیسوانت را آواره کرد؟
و چین های ریز چادرت را
در باران سوزاندند؟
کسی که بر جنازهٔ نوجوانئ ام کفن پیچید
شبیه خودم بود
با فریادی که نکرده بودم
و بلندتر بود

حالا به سهم خودم از استخوان هایم بیشتر معترضم
و خاکستری که از حماسه های سرد پوسید
و خون که از باران های موسمی
خودش را پنهان می کند
و می ترسم
از کسی که بیاید
و تکه های تورا
از این جاده جمع کند
و دروغ بگوید /
که باز هم تو را دوباره
در خواب پروانه ها
سوزانده اند

۱۳۸۴

A YOUNG STREET-VENDOR THINKS OF IMPORTED GOODS

You will not be convinced
if I tell you
about stars or about fresh water lilies
      infusing the lagoon's lazy muscles
      with their vivid wishes.
The sparrows sing for you—
like me—
of these modest delights
but you
risk your beloved glass fears
      in a field of stones.

Let me tell you then
how once more
      down the length of the noisy street
for the seventh day in a row
      an insistent child staggers through the bus,
        trying to sell her pack of gum,
          a life spun from pockets
            and palms.

I suppose this house still smells like rain
and mud home afternoons
and you
      have grown used to painting over
        the dirt-streaks of scarcity with laughter.

I get off the bus,
      walk,
         and imagine you reaching
the last row of the chess board.

تو که قانع نمی شوی

اگر از ستاره بگویم
یا نیلوفران تازه ای
که به عضلات تنبل مرداب
آرزوهای زنده تزریق می کنند
گنجشک ها برای تو می خوانند
مثل من /
که دلخوشی های ساده ام را
تو اما
دلهره های شیشه ای عزیزت را
کنار این سنگ ها چیده ای

ساده /
تمام می شوم
و دوباره /
حجم شلوغ خیابان
سماجت دخترکی که برای هفتمین روز متوالی
بستهٔ آدامسش را
در میان ملی بس می چرخاند
و می چرخید
همهٔ زندگی را /
در جیبها و دستها

به گمانم این خانه بوی باران می دهد هنوز
و عصرهای کاهگلی
و تو /
که عادت کرده ای هر روز
خنده هایت را بر بی چیزی رگ های خاک بریزی

پیاده می شوم /
پیاده می روم
و پیاده خیال می کنم
که تو به خانه های آخر شطرنج
می رسی

Now, there is sky
and long ropes of rain
while the young street-vendor
still thinks of imported goods.

(2005)

حالا آسمان هست
ریسمان بلند باران هست
اگر چه دستفروش جوان
هنوز هم به کالای وارده فکر می کند

۱۳۸۴

AND VIOLET TUNES OF LAWLESSNESS

And the violet tunes of lawlessness
are in a mood
to make the wind's wild violins
      hope for eternal insanity.

A simple, distant secret,
familiar with the breath of skin,
      makes space in my poems
      for all the suns ever set
and leaves them behind
on an orange-tinged leaf.

Do you think I could remember
over these long years,
      long distances

someone who followed me
from the perfect surface of the water
        who was left behind
      who left me
      in the footprints
      that conclude their journey
        in the sand?

And after that
from silver desert,
like the warm-meets-cold of wind, inside me
      the gale stirred from pieces of me
        meeting, changing places with
          the shapelessness
          I do not know.

و آوازهای بنفش بی قانون

در نی‌ای
که ویولون های وحشی باد را
به جنونی ابدی امیدوار می کند

چه راز ساده و دوری!
آشنا به تنفس پوستی
که همه غروب ها را
در شعرم جا می دهد
و جا می ماند
لای یک برگ نارنجی

یادم آمده است انگار
نرسیده به این سال ها /
دورِ دور

کسی که از سطح سادهٔ آب پا به پایم آمد /
جا مانده است

جایم گذاشته
در رد پایم
که در شن تمام می شود

و سپس باد /
و سپس های پس از باد
و همچنان های همشکل همیشه

می دانی
باد را
از بیابان های نقره ای آغاز کرده ام
از جابجایی تکه های خودم
با بی شکل تکه هایی
که نمی دانم

I guess this winding anxiety
was threaded through generations
by my own fingers.

They prolong you—
on and on,

following from the song
that blocks my path

or is it you who hinders me?

or maybe I lost the way
                    to you
                    to the song
                    to the self...

Here, right here
the heavy rancor of stars
restores memory.

Beauty... what beauty in genuine sorrow!

But why can't I remember
        where in the story you regain consciousness
        and did the wind
                lure you
                into the viscous haze of today?

Why can't I recall the words
of the agreement that said you would
        come,
        stay,
        narrate your smiling tales?

این پریشانی /
به گمانم موروثی شده است
در این نسل ها
که از زایش انگشتانم شکل گرفته اند

ادامه ات می دهند
ادامه / ادامه

ادامه از
ترنمی که راهم نمی دهد در خود
یا خودت
که راه نمی دهی

و شاید خودم
که راه نیافته در تو
در ترنم
در خود...
همینجاست

همینجا
که بغض های سنگین ستاره /
یادم را می آورد
چه زیبایی محزون معتبری!
چرا به یادم نمی آید /
کجای روایت /
به هوش آمدی
و باد
تو را
در بخار غلیظ قرن وسوسه کرد؟

این اتفاق که بیایی
که بمانی /
که راوی لبخند های خودت باشی
که راوی لبخند های خودت باشی

Why do I still doubt
whether you were revived at all?

Now
living in this homelessness
my arms can't reach each other

Night, borne on your shoulders,
        leaks from recollection
nor could I find—no—
a companion to reminisce with.

Can you recall where
I lost you

or where
in the soil my fingerprints
            were?

Or perhaps those weren't prints, just

            a remnant

of the moon's shadow.

(2005)

چرا به یادم نمی آید؟

چرا به هوش نیامده ای
انگار؟

حالا
سکونت در این آوارگی ها /
هیچ
دست هایم نمی رسد به هم / هم
به کنار
شب که از هوش میرود
روی شانه های تو / هم...
کسی به فکر این انگار های به یاد آورد
نمی شود
اصلا
اصلا
به یاد می آوری

کجا
که مانده بود گودی انگشت هایم
در خاک؟

و یادم هست که خاک
تنها سایهٔ ممکن ماه بود

۱۳۸۴

NILUFAR NIKSEAR

نیلوفر نیک سیر

(1987-)

Nilufar Niksear (Nīlūfar Nīksear) was born in Kabul in 1987, where she lived and studied until 6th grade. When the Taliban invaded the capital, she and her family moved to Herat. She finished her schooling in Herat after the Taliban's defeat, and continued on to study Persian Language and Literature at Herat University, graduating with her bachelor's in 2010. She first became involved with the Herat Literary Society when she was in 10th grade, and has been an active member ever since. Niksear's work has been featured in numerous publications and anthologies, including *Kojāhā hanūz estāda-and* (*Where Do They Now Stand?* 2008), Īnjā *chahārshanbe ast* (*It is Wednesday Here,* 2010), and Īnjā *naguftahā ast* (*There is Much Left Unsaid Here,* 2010). Her first collection of poems is forthcoming.

Nilufar Niksear. Photo courtesy of Nilufar Niksear.

Cover of Īnjā *chahārshanbe ast* (*It is Wednesday Here*), one of the anthologies featuring Nilufar Niksear. Photo by Farzana Marie

Note on the Translations

This selection of three ghazals and one free verse poem by Nilufar Niksear is representative of her body of work, which features mainly formal verse, especially ghazals. Translating forms like the ghazal always requires balancing form and meaning in the process of seeking a new music and rhythm in the new language. Niksear's poems, though, lend themselves to a certain freedom in formal interpretation, as she herself experiments and stretches the confines of the form. For example, in the first ghazal included here, she breaks the "radif" rule: the traditional repetition of the same word concluding each *beit* (two lines of poetry on the page). She does not use the repeated *radif,* but rather uses rhyming end-words (*tekrār, diwār, bezār, āzār)* instead. In this respect, the English version of the poem lent itself to a closer approximation of the form than in Persian Dari, simply because of the versatility of the word *repeat,* and the way that it contributed to the poem's emotional emphasis.

A thought-provoking challenge in translating Niksear is her use of allusions. Nilufar Niksear has read a wide variety of poets and her Facebook posts frequently include Persian translations of poets like Wisława Szymborska and Charles Bukowski alongside classical Persian giants like Hafez and Rudaki as well as modern Iranian and Afghan masters like Ahmad Shamlū, Simin Behbāhāni, and Qahār Āsi. In her third ghazal included in this selection, she writes the following:

گفتی که هفت شهر غزل در صدای اوست
وقتی برای خستگیم خواب می سرود

His voice held the tune of seven cities of lyrics
when he sang sleep for my weariness.

This couplet refers, in all likelihood, to a well-known couplet by Mowlana (Jelaluddin Rumi) and describes another Persian Sufi poet, Farid ud-Din Attar of Nishapur, this way:

Attar has traversed the seven cities of Love,
While we have barely turned down the first street.

In his poetic allegory, *The Conference of the Birds* (*Manteq At-tair*), Attar describes seven valleys of love on a quest that thousands of birds undertake in hopes of reaching the highest peak, Mount Qaf, and the legendary ultimate being and ruler who presides there, the Simurgh. After an arduous and perilous journey on which many die and many others give up, only thirty birds arrive at their destination to succeed in seeking an audience with the great Simurgh. They are kept waiting, then ultimately find in a shocking turn of events that the Simurgh is actually a representation of themselves (*si murgh* literally means *thirty birds* in Persian).

Thus, Niksear's twist on the "seven cities of love," turning it into the "seven cities of lyric," suggests potential interpretations of this poem beyond a simple love lyric. The excruciating, all-encompassing journey through seven cities or seven valleys of love begins in pursuit of the divine Beloved, the ultimate prince or ruler. But the revelation that concludes this journey hints that after weathering this quest, the most profound discovery is of your own features in the face of the Beloved. Perhaps, then, Niksear is reaching here toward the idea that the pursuit of authentic love may result in a deepened self-recognition and awareness.

GHAZAL 1

I am tired of repeat, repeat, and again *repeat*:
lay head on wall's shoulder...*repeat*—
life, love, and comfort leave a bad taste
so suffer this stubborn sting alone...*repeat*.
Torment grips me all the way down to the deep
as the death-dagger-blood-reel continually *repeats*.
Hear the ailing narrator of this bitter tale,
the story life builds breath by breath...*repeat*.
Believe just for once, how bad it hurts—
don't leave beside me an empty seat.

غزل

من خسته از تکرار تکرار و هی تکرار
سر می نهم با خود، برشانه ی دیوار
رنج مداوم را، هی میکشم تنها
از زنده گی از عشق، از دلخوشی بیزار
هی مرگ هی دشنه، هی قطره های خون
تا عمق احساسم، در گیر یک آزار
این زنده گی هردم، یك قصه میسازد
راوی این تلخی، تنها منِ بیمار
گفتم کنارم را، خالی نکن از خود
تنها تو باور کن، درد مرا یک بار!

At Night in This Empty Neighborhood

At night in this empty neighborhood
delirium hits the side-street of the mind
a dead person walks inside me
my path wanes.
At night in this empty neighborhood
the village was drowned in bullets
blood still flowed up
to the edge of a house that was crushed.
Waiting, drowning in my own silence
I sit and watch the road
the street has swallowed your footprints
I see a well on your path
I am tired of myself—help me
to accelerate my death a little,
to draw nightmares again
on the walls of my brain.
The house is burning once more in a fever
in the house's elongated dreams
a woman sits over there with her fears
fear of the screams of her disease
At night I brim with pain
All night soaking in delirium
my heart beats completely cold
like a hammer and anvil
the hour swells with pain's mass
night is gone
the howl of a dog that has been kicked
is everywhere dispersed.

در شب این حوالی خالی

کوچه ذهنش دچار هذیانست
مرد ه ي راه میرود در من
راه من راه رو به پایانست
درشب این حوالي خالي
دهکده غرق تیرباران شد
همچنان خون رو به بالا رفت
تا لب خانه ای که ویران شد
منتظر غرق در سکوت خودم
مي نشینم و راه مي بینم
جاده بلعید رد پایت را
سر راه تو چاه مي بینم
از خودم خسته ام تو یاري کن
مرگ خود را کمي جلو بکشم
روي دیوار هاي ذهنم باز
کمي کابوس هاي نو بکشم
خانه در تب دوباره میسوزد
خانه در خوابهاي کشدارش
آن طرف زن نشسته در ترسش
ترس از جیغ هاي بیمارش
شب تماما درون یك دردم
شب تماما درون هذیانها
قلب من میتپد سراسر سرد
مثل پتکي بروي سندانها
ساعت از حجم درد لبریزاست
شب به پایان رسیده تا آخر
زوزه هاي سگي لگد خورده
منتشر گشته است سرتاسر.

91

GHAZAL 2

Sediment of sentiment, waves of lyric flow
in the pond of your hands, along with the flow
of hundreds of tomorrow-windows, hundreds of springs,
hundreds of colorful kindnesses and sweet anxieties flow
in the depth of your gaze as the image of honey flows.
In your whispers I am lost and found—
in this lost me a sea of contradiction flows.
It's as if the sensation of you fills me with each breath,
like a lyric this lovely sense of you flows.

غزل

در بر که دستانت احساس و غزل جاری
صد روزنه ی فردا، صد ماه حمل جاری
صد عاطفهٔ رنگین، صد دلهُرهٔ شیرین
در عمق نگاه تو تصویر عسل جاری
در زمزمه های تو گم گشته و پیدایم
در این من گم گشته دریای جدل جاری
با هر نفسم گویی پر می شوم از حسّت
این حسِ قشنگ تو در من چو غزل جاری

GHAZAL 3

He would sing a pure ghazal just with his eyes,
sing water to my life's parched times.
When night dragged its gloom over my mood
how easily he would sing me moonlight.
His voice held the tune of seven cities of lyrics
when he sang sleep for my weariness.
Nightly, he would stand restlessly outside
romancing me with serenade of rain and garden.
Now I rely on memory—where is he
who sang pure lyrics for me?

غزل

او با نگاه خود غزلی ناب می سرود
در خشک سال زندگیم آب می سرود
وقت که شب تمام وجودم به بر کشید
او بهر من ز چه ساده ز مهتاب می سرود
گفتی که هفت شهر غزل در صدای اوست
وقتی برای خستگیم خواب می سرود
آواز عاشقانه باران و باغ را
هر شب کنار پنجره بی تاب می سرود
اینک کنار خاطر خود تکیه کرده ام
کو آن که بهر من غزلی ناب می سرود؟

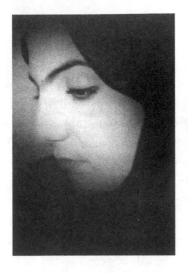

FERESHTA NILAB SAHEL NOORZAYI

فرشته نیلاب ساحل نورزایی

(1977-2010)

"Fereshta" Nilab Sahel Noorzayi (Fereshta Nilāb Sāhel Nūrzāyī), cousin to Nadia Anjuman, was born in 1977 to a Herati family in Kabul. She entered Herat University in 2002 and graduated from the English Literature department with honors. She went on to work as a teacher and administrator at a local school, but in early 2010 a strange thing happened. As recounted in the biography printed in the small volume of her collected poems, her family says she had a dream forty days before her death she would be taking a trip to a new, eternal country. Forty days after this, by the account, she died in her sleep on February 25th, 2010. Her book of poems, titled *Wīdā'* *(Farewell)*, was printed that same year, following her death.

Fereshta Nilab Sahel Noorzayi, from page in *Wīdā'*.

Book cover of *Wīdā'* by Fereshta Nilab Sahel Noorzayi.

Photos by Farzana Marie.

Note on the Translations

All of the poems included here are from Noorzayi's book of poems, *Wīdā'* (*Farewell*). In the collection, Noorzayi demonstrates mastery of various Persian poetic forms, including the *masnavi* (rhyming couplets), *ghazal*, and free verse (*sher-e safeyd*). The ghazal is the most predominant form Fereshta uses in her collection, so I have included several here. In translation of these formal poems, I have prioritized the meaning and flow of the language over strict adherence to a formal structure in English. In the poem, "But I Couldn't," I use a refrain that recurs in a similar way to the repeated end-word or phrase (*radeef*) of the ghazal, to give a sense, however imperfect, of the Persian Dari rhythm. Here, as in the poem "These Days," where I repeat the word "us" as a gesture toward the ghazal, I have chosen not adhere to other rules of this form, such as the convention that each couplet be a grammatically complete unit. The same applies to "Farewell," which is the final poem in Noorzayi's collection and likewise concludes the selection here. In "Farewell," the end-word, "go," recurs seven times, just as it does in Fereshta's original with *rawam* (a form of "I go"). In punctuating the poem this way, the translation seeks to echo the original by underscoring the poem's central impulse (*go go go*).

In "Sincerity," the translation departs from repeated end-words, instead emphasizing assonance and internal or slant rhymes like stone-toned/soak, shut/caught, and wound/move to build a rhythmic mood. The name and theme of this particular poem also presented an interesting challenge in translation. The poem's title in Dari, *Yakrangī*, literally means "one-colored-ness" or "of one color" and has connotations of friendship, sincerity, closeness, harmony, good faith, truthfulness, and authenticity as well as a rich literary history. (By contrast, *dū-rāngī*, or two-colored-ness means hypocrisy, duplicity, or having "two faces.") By invoking color, the title interacts with the poem in multi-layered ways as the poet plays with various shades and hues in the text. While I use the title "Sincerity" to most accurately reflect the meaning of the word, elsewhere in the body of the poem I use the phrase "True Colors" to reflect *yakrangī* in a different way by combining the ideas of forthrightness and color.

Another clever (but difficult to translate) case of wordplay occurs in two of the selected poems, "These Days" and "Sincerity," and involves the use of the poet's name, *Sahel*, in the last one to two lines of the poem. While this harkens to a Persian literary convention of self-address or self-reference by the poet in forms such as the ghazal, here Noorzayi is also playing on the meaning of *Sahel*, which is "shore." In "These Days" the double-meaning is clear in Dari when poet says "The sea overwhelms Sahel." Likewise, in "Sincerity," she refers to the beloved as *darya-e man* (my sea / my ocean), asking for pity on *Sahel*, (the shore). In the English, I chose to preserve the word Sahel, as it clearly intends a reference to the poet's name, hoping this note might further enhance the appreciation of the artfulness of the poem in Persian Dari.

Along with the four ghazals, I have included one short poem in free verse. *Khat-e surkh* or "Red Line" is the penultimate poem in Fereshta's collection. Although simple, this poem plays with a number of compelling ideas and images in a very small space. Arranged as a combined self-interrogation and self-admonition, the poem's speaker decries the crossing of the "red line," imagined here as topographical feature like a precipice. By using the word "line," however, the poet implies written lines as well, communicating underlying tensions about writing poetry in the context of many societal taboos in speaking, writing, and other public acts. It begs the question: what is the "red line" the poet (especially the female poet) dare not cross, lest she be "erased," prevented from writing further?

BUT I COULDN'T

I thought I would adorn my world bright,
grow joy a place of honor in my life—
but I couldn't.
I said I would straighten my back
bent by a bruised history
but I couldn't.
I wanted to trade my canvas clothes for silk,
with thoughts of you to thrill me
but I couldn't.
I said, today my resolve is firm:
I will expand my heart into an ocean
but I couldn't.
I thought I would give my love a glimpse
of my heart's secrets, uncover his
but I couldn't.
I longed to loose this tangled tongue
in his ravishing presence
but I couldn't.
Love-struck in this revolt, I swore
I would exile him from my thoughts
but I couldn't.
I wanted to stand in protest against
life's cruelty, my lover's rejection
but I couldn't.
His oppression dragged on, my fortitude faltered,
I meant to shout for justice, demand a redress of our woes,
but I couldn't.

اما نشد

گفتم دنیایم بزم آرا کنم، اما نشد
ساحه دلزندگی کبرا کنم، اما نشد
گفتم آسیب زمان بسیار دیدم باز هم
این خمیده قامتم بالا کنم، اما نشد
خواستم تا در خیالت بهر شادی دلم
جامهٔ کرباس را دیبا کنم، اما نشد
با خودم گفتم امروز قاطع است تصمیم من
دل وسیع گردانم و دریا کنم، اما نشد
گفتم حتما دلبرم از راز دل آگه کنم
راز و اسرار دلش پیدا کنم، اما نشد
دل تمنا داشت تا من در حضور دلربا
این زبان بسته را گویا کنم، اما نشد
چون شدم شیدا ز شورش عهد کردم با خودم
دورش از فکرو هم از سودا کنم، اما نشد
از ستم های زمان و از جفای دلبرم
خواستم هنگامه ای بر پا کنم، اما نشد
بسکه جورش را کشیدم، طاقت من طاق شد
قصد کردم داد و واویلا کنم، اما نشد

THESE DAYS

These days, their plagues oppress us
with tyranny, toil, and why?
No sign of kindness, mercy,
or compassion appears to us.
Time tears down the heart's
love-carved roof beams, exposes us
to naked sky, the overseer
of these midnight doubts and sighs.
The age has left a souvenir for us
(even as it conjures new sufferings):
a sickly body and pain without remedy.
The world's vicious riptide leaves us
no hope of this night-journey ever reaching morning:
a ship broken, the captain intact.
It is impossible for us
to straighten our backs when our legacy
is a chest-full of regrets. We were crushed,
and time's best advice for us?
Get used to my cruelty, it burns but you can learn
to tolerate the burning, it said to us.
So we buried our cries in our hearts, buried our voices
in tombs of tired throats. What's left for us
but to imagine the dreams that might have come true for us?
The sea overwhelms Sahel, whose cries resound;
as footsteps fade, she left her tears to us.

روزگار

ز افعال زمان برما جفا ماند
بلا ماند وکفا ماند و چرا ماند

عطوفت و مروت نیست پیدا
کجا آثاری از جود و سخا ماند

محبت است ستون خانه ی دل
ستون ها ریختند بر جا سما ماند

سر شک دیده و آه شبانگاه
رهایمان نکرد تا انتها ماند

به یادگار از ستم های زمانه
تن رنجور و درد بی دوا ماند

به گرداب تلاطم زای گیتی
شکست کشتی وسالم ناخدا ماند

نداشت این شام تاریک صبح در پی
به دل ها حسرت باد صبا ماند

نشد گاهی که قامت راست سازیم
ز بس کوبیده شد این انحنا ماند

به هر جور زمان باید صبوری
برای سوختن ساختن سزا ماند

شده مدفون فغان در سینهٔ ما
گلوی خسته را خاموش صدا ماند

دریاب عالم ز کام دل رسیدن
فقط رویای نا پیدا به ما ماند

گذاشت دریا سرش بر دوش «ساحل»
گریست و رفت و اشک او بجا ماند

SINCERITY

Why do you paint my dawn stone-toned, darling,
letting me soak in the wet pain of it as if dagger-pierced?
Hunter-dear, the snare of your eyes has snapped shut,
my heart's ankle caught, what need is there now
for your crossbow?
Where would I run to treat my fatal wound
that you move to trap me again in this abyss?
Everyone says you mean to use magic
as if your previous witchcraft had fallen short of its aim.
What might have been, my cruel one,
had you lit the candle of your true colors
let the sun rise once in my black hours?
Take pity on this bloodied half-corpse,
the one you glance at sideways
after wounding red unto death.
Your oppression rises up the ranks;
you've rained fiery dread a long time,
finally crushing me with one of its embers.
Your position will not be endangered, my ocean,
if you look kindly on Sahel's suffering.

یکرنگی

چرا بر صبح من جانا تو رنگ اخدر اندازی؟
کزان دردی کنم احساس که گویی خنجر اندازی

بدام چشم تو صیاد! چنان گیر است پای دل
که حاجت نیست بهرش تو، کمند دیگر اندازی

کجا این ناقۀ عشقت صحت یاب گشته است کامل
که بار دیگری خواهی در این ورطه در اندازی

همه گویند ترا قصد است، بیافزایی به جادویت
مگر کم بوده افسونت که طرح اسحر اندازی؟

چه میشد ای ستم کارا! که از فانوس یکرنگی
بر این شام سیاه من، طلوع از هر اندازی

بکن رحمی بر این بسمل که در خون می تپد هردم
که او را با ناوک چشمت به موت احمر اندازی

مقام و منزل جورت رود بالا و بالاتر
شرر ریزی دلم چندی ولی حال اخگر اندازی

تو ای دریای من! شأنت، شکوهت کم نمیگردد
به حال «ساحل» بشکسته دل گر منظر اندازی

RED LINE

Why, oh why
would you step on this red line,
this precipice?
Pull your foot away—quick!
Lest the abyss
erase you.

خط سرخ!

ای وای!
چرا بر روی خط سرخ پا نهی؟
پایت بکش کنار!
این پرتگاه ترا
نابود میکند!

FAREWELL

I want to leave this "home" and go
to the grasslands, pack up and go
to a place I imagine soaked in the scent of peace—
no? If that land does not exist I will go
to the dust-scented desert, go
no matter how many times they bind
my feet, the ties will rot and I will go
in search of a country of lovely souls.
These colorful clothes did no good, I will go
now robed in white. The lovers call: *come!*
The time of farewells has come and I must go!

وداع

خواهم کزین دیار بسوی چمن روم
من رخت بسته ام وزین انجمن روم
عطر دل انگیزی نوازد مرا مشام
آن عطر، عطری نیست بغیری سمن روم
هرچند تنابها به پایم که بسته اند
خود پاره میشود همه آن رسن روم
انجا که دیده ام بسی نیکو سیرتان
لیک من مکان خلق تماما حسن روم
این جامه های رنگ نزیبد دگر مرا
من جامه سفید بباید به تن روم
آن عاشقان پاک صدایم زنند، بیا!
وقت وداع رسیده و باید که من روم

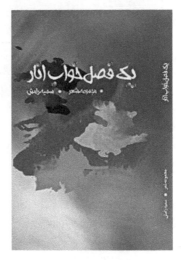

SOMAIA RAMISH

سمیه رامش

(1986-)

Somaia Ramish (Somaia Rāmish) was born in 1986 in Tehran, Iran, where she first became acquainted with Persian literature. After the fall of the Taliban, she returned to Afghanistan and her family's native city of Herat, where she became actively involved with Herat Literary Society's Youth Association. Her first poetry collection, *Kamī barāye khudam (A Little Bit for Me)* was published in 2008 by Fedāyi-e Herawī Press. In 2009, the poet published a book of interviews with Herati poets including Fariba Haidari. A second poetry collection released in 2013 is titled *Yak Fasl-e Khāb-e Anār (A Season of Pomegranate Dreams)*. Ms. Ramish founded a social-cultural organization called *Naw-Andishān* (New Thinkers) and serves as an elected member of Herat's provincial council.

Somaia Ramish, used by permission.

Cover of *Yak Fasl-e Khāb-e Anār* by Somaia Ramish, used by permission.

Note on the Translations

With the exception of "For Nadia Anjuman," the poems in this selection come from Somaia Ramish's latest book, *A Season of Pomegranate Dreams,* dedicated to "the young women of my country who, moment by moment, have lived death."[2] Indeed, many of the poems in this collection directly address social issues, particularly issues related to violence against women, underage or forced marriage, poverty, and the impacts of extremism and war. This selection includes poems that exemplify Somaia's skill for irony, along with a range of existential musings. The poems also engage with socio-political themes characteristic of the poet's larger body of work. One difference in all the poems between the original and the translation is that none of the poems in Persian Dari have titles (they are numbered in the book), and have remained untitled here. The English titles are my additions, in order to identify the poems.

Somaia Ramish is a poet with international influences, beginning with her early years in a neighboring country, and her poems bear this out. In "The Girl Who Sold God," as in many of her poems, Ramish uses loan-words from other languages in phrases like "secular trees" and "democratic thoughts." While these ideas might have been expressed in different ways, the cognates in Dari (*sukūlār* and *demākrāt*) were preserved. This type of decision attempts to shorten the distance between the original connotations and those of the translation, whereas in other places I opted to lengthen that distance slightly in favor of a crisper sound-image capture. In "Load Poems like Guns," the literal repeated phrase Somaia's poem repeats is closer to, "Fill your poems with gunpowder." In this case, I chose a shorter phrase that more directly invokes the same image or action in English.

The poem "And the Word Null" questions the meaningfulness of language and writing, playing with slight variations on

---

2   Dedication page of *Yak Fasl-e Khāb-e Anār.*

word-order and sounds to arrive at different meanings and heighten effects. In translation, I aimed for similar effects, sometimes sacrificing precise meaning for a more resonant sound that more closely reflected the original. For example, at the end of the poem, Somaia uses three words with similar sounds: *hich* (none/nothing) *pooch* (empty/hollow/void) and *hashw* (redundant/superfluous). In the translation, I kept the pattern of three essentially nothing-words, repetitive and ironic in their repetition. I used *null, dust,* and *superfluous* in an attempt to represent a similar sound-pattern as well as a sense of nothingness.

In the same poem, Ramish incorporates religious references to explore the relationship between language and the divine. The most prominent is her use of the phrase from the Gospel of John in the New Testament or *Injil*: "That in the beginning was the word..." In its original context, the phrase is a reference to the identification of the Messiah Jesus (Isa-e Masih) as the *word* or breath of God in human flesh. The first line of the poem could also be a Qur'anic reference: here it is "You said, *write*" instead of the instruction famously received by the Prophet Mohammad to *recite*. By making these references, Somaia draws on iconic language-oriented human interactions with the divine to question where the importance of *words* begins and ends. In the process of translation, I hoped to preserve this sense of inquiry, of stirring the reader to question: *Does language, in fact, matter? What significance, in reality, do words possess—does this poem I am reading right now matter?*

THE GIRL WHO SOLD GOD

Last night in the streets someone put God up for sale
on a vendor's cart.
Prospective buyers came by as she called,
   Buy God, Buy God,
      spread his fragrance everywhere.
That's what the girl who sold God said.

This city is filled with secular trees,
monkeys who speak with accents of women and trees.
    People here sow fortunes they don't have
for love;
their blithe smiles drunk
on happiness all night.

My hair has breathed as long as my days.
Here, even the sun's slaps are pleasant
and I have reconciled with bright colors:
reds
yellows
greens.
My hue is a hopeful white,
my democratic thoughts having forgotten that this
is a town where people fall in love with the smells of both
poverty and ginger.

(2010)

دیشب کسی خدایش را میان کوچه ای حراج کرد

روی یک گاری
مردم آمدند تا خدا بخرند
«همه جا بوی خدا میدهد»
این را دختری میگفت، که خدا را فروخت.

اینجا شهریست با درخت های سکولار
و میمون هایی که لهجه ی درخت و زن را میفهمند
اینجا مردم تمام ثروتی که ندارند را عشق میکارند
و تمام شب مستِ مست
لبخند!

موهایم به اندازه تمام عمر نفس کشیده و قد
اینجا
سیلی آفتاب هم تجربه قشنگی ست
من با رنگها آشتی شده ام
با سرخ ها
زردها
سبز ها
سفیدِ سفیدم
دموکرات فکر میکنم
ویادم رفته این شهر مردمی ست که بابوی فقر و زنجبیل هم عاشق
میشوند!

۲۰۱۰

And the Word Null

You said, *write*
You said, tell me of the miracle of
words, you said
I became a stream of speech
for you   of words from the beginning.
That in the beginning was the word and the word was
the beginning.
But I knew nothing
of the end
of becoming   nothing
of being   nothing.
I said, how can I write your non-existence?

I spit myself onto a page
a painting that sent
the alphabet to its death.
In this way a thousand-and-nothing ancestors
of a generation of nothing-becomers
face ruin.
Your scandal
or mine?
And existence is everything that from the beginning
was my likeness   the painting
was the likeness   of my painting
that wrote nothing more.

And the word *null*
and the word *dust*
and the word *superfluous*.

گفتی بنویس

گفتی از اعجاز کلمه بگو

گفتی...

جاری شدم برایت

از کلام

از کلمه از آغاز

«که در آغاز کلمه بود و کلمه آغاز بود»

و - من انجام را نمیدانستم

هیچ شدن را

هیچ بودن را

گفتم چطور بنویسم نبودنت را

تف کردم خودم را به روی یک کاغذ

شکل یک نقاشی

که مرگ میفرستاد بر الفبا

بر اجداد هزار و هیچم یک نسل

به تبار هیچ شدگان این شکلی!

چه افتضاحی از من

از تو

و هستی هرآنچه از آغاز

که شبیه من نقاشی

که شبیه نقاشی من

که دیگر ننوشت

و کلمه هیچ

کلمه پوچ

کلمه حشو!

Another Looking Glass, Another Lie

Another looking glass
another lie
and I
with my inverted smiles
      practice proper manners

since the world reviles
      my waywardness
      my repetitive mistakes
I scatter my lips
my smile
my glance
      across the broken glass

how lovely it would have been
had my excuses never awoken.

باز هم دروغ

آیینه

من

لبخند های وارونه

و تمرین مرتب شدن!

پراکنده گی ام چون فحشی

در جهان

در اشتباه مکرر یک تکرار

لبانم را

لبخندم را

نگاهم را

تقسیم میکنم در آیینه ای شکسته

و

معذورم بدار که نمیشود مرتب زیبا بود!

LOAD POEMS LIKE GUNS

Load poems like guns—
war's geography calls you
to arms.
The enemy has no signs,
counter-signs,
colors
signals
symbols!
Load poems like guns—
each moment is loaded
with bombs
bullets
blasts
death-sounds—
death and war
don't follow rules
you can make your pages into white flags
a thousand times
but swallow your words, say no more.
Load your poems—
your body—
your thoughts—
like guns.
The schoolhouses of war rise up
within you.
Maybe you
are next.

شعر هایت را با باروت پُر کن

باید مسلح باشی
جغرافیای جنگ اینجاست
هیچ نشانی
رنگی
نشانه ای
دشمن ندارد!
شعر هایت را با باروت پُر کن
هر لحظه توپی
تفنگی
انفجاری
مرگی
هیچ قانونی ندارد مرگ
هیچی قانونی ندارد جنگ
هزار بار هم ورق های سفید را بیرق کنی
کلماتت را قورت دهی و هیچ نگویی باز هم...
شعر هایت را با باروت پُر کن
تنت را
اندیشه ات را
مدرسه های جنگ از درونت به پا میخیزند
شاید نفر بعدی خودت باشی!

121

FOR NADIA ANJUMAN

The sky died
for the wind that split open its chest

We all died for you
though fate's sleight of hand snuck you from us

And you smiled from the sky
for us
and for the moments we carry away
from our memories.

تقدیم به نادیا انجمن

باد که سینه آسمان را شکافت
آسمان برای خودش مُرد
دست روزگار که تو را از ما چید
همه برای تو مُردیم
و تو از آسمان خندیدی
برای ما
و برای لحظه ای که ما خود را هم از یاد می بریم.

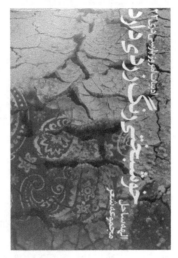

ELAHA SAHEL

الهه ساحل

(1984-)

Elaha Sahel (Elāha Sāhel) was born in 1984 in Kabul, Afghanistan. She holds a bachelor's degree from Herat University in Persian Literature and her work has appeared in several anthologies including *Haq bā tamāme durūgh-hā ast* (*Lies Have the Right of Way*, 2005), *Īnjā chahārshanbe ast* (*It Is Wednesday Here*, 2010), and a large anthology of Herati poets, both male and female, called *Kojāhā hanūz estāda-and* (*Where Do They Now Stand?* 2008). Sahel's first collection of poems, entitled *Khoshbakhtī rang-e zardi dārad* (*Happiness Is the Color Yellow*), was published in 2010 in Herat, where she lives with her husband and two children. She is an active member of Herat's Youth Literary Association and an outspoken advocate and organizer for human rights in Afghanistan, especially women's rights.

Elaha Sahel. Used by permission.

Book cover of *Khoshbakhtī rang-e zardi dārad* by Elaha Sahel.
Photo by Farzana Marie

Note on the Translations

The playfulness of Elaha Sahel's poetry only serves to accentuate the seriousness of the topics she takes on, often condensing monumental ideas or problems into a few words, a single image. She uses a variety of styles and experiments including micro-poetry (several examples of which are included here) to express significant, often socio-political, themes. Unlike Nadia Anjuman or Muzhgan Faramanesh, one rarely sees classical-form poems in Elaha's notebooks; rather, one is more likely to see single letters floating down the page or short phrases dancing in a circle.

The challenge in translating a poet like Elaha often lies in capturing the right tone in a very short space. "Painting," for instance, conveys in three lines and a single startling image the calamity of man's obsession with violence, his creation (as depicted in the weapon painted on canvas) of new ways to destroy. The blindfolded bird portrays the shock of the innocent, being shaken to the point of confronting this reality. The poem might have been titled "Art of War," but this makes too many assumptions, as war is not the only kind of violence possibly implied here. What Elaha does in three lines (and no title), I have attempted to capture in four.

All the poems in this selection are excerpted from *Happiness Is the Color Yellow,* which is concerned with a host of social issues, many of them personal to the poet, living as a bold and ambitious woman in a society that does not always appreciate these qualities in her gender. In "Clean Skirts," Elaha makes fun of a place "where even mountains / wear skirts stitched to their heels," yet the tone is only half-mockery. Near despair, the speaker wonders, "And how could the sound of smiling / spread across this stained century?" The poem ends with a reference to the famous Sufi poet-saint of Herat, Khāja Abdullah Ansari, buried in the *Kābirgāh* cemetery outside the city (where, incidentally, Elaha and I went together to visit Nadia Anjuman's grave in 2013). There is little choice, it seems, other than to try and be remembered as a "saint." While some other reference might have been more accessible for English-language readers, I have chosen to preserve this one, with this note as an aid.

Some of the symbolism in Elaha's poems also provided an interesting challenge in translation. In "Ode to My Earrings," for instance, the poet uses the phrase "happiness is the color yellow," which is also the title of her collection. In a conversation about this idea, Elaha pointed out that she was inverting the expected, since in Dari happiness might *not* be associated with the color yellow as it would in English (like sunshine, or perhaps in American culture, a Walmart smiley face). Although a subtlety, in Afghan and Persian culture the color yellow can be associated with separation and sickness. For example, an ancient tradition that comes from Zoroastrianism is still practiced by many Afghans and Iranians around the New Year, or *Nauruz*, in March. On the Tuesday before the spring equinox, people kindle several fires on the ground, leaping over them while calling out, *"Zardīye man az tū, surkhīye tū az man,"* suggesting a trade with the fire: *"My yellows* (sickness, decay) *for your reds"* (life, health, vibrancy). While I could have used something more intuitively surprising in English, such as "Happiness Is the Color Blue," the layering of ideas in Elaha's formulation was too rich to eliminate.

While "Ode to My Earrings" is an example of Ms. Sahel's more exuberant, lighthearted poems, many of her works also deal directly with subjects of war, conflict, and injustice. In "Protest," the poet utilizes a refrain that echoes the seeming never-ending-ness of conflict after conflict: "It keeps going, / going, / going on." The poem points to the generational impact of growing up in war, and the role that education plays either in reinforcing violence or (and this part is implied) presenting alternatives. "When the neighbor's kid continues / to learn "b" for battlefield / and "j" for jihad, / how will we be able to breathe / through the gunpowder?" The poem has arrived at a dark place, but the end presents a twist: war is not the only thing that goes on.

SINFUL SKIRTS

Sinful-skirted girls
still think like virgins
        about the night

and from underneath
their umbrellas look for one pure,
transparent droplet.

Cloud-skirted mountains
quench chastity's thirst
drop
by drop.

And how could the sound of smiling
spread across this stained century?

Here, where even mountains
wear skirts stitched to their heels

the last resort is a tombstone
etched with the words,
Resting Place of the Saint, Khāja Ansār.

دامنه های عاصی

دامنه های عاصی
هنوز باکره می اندیشند
شب را

و
زیر چتر باران
زلالی اعتماد میجویند

دامنه های ابری
تشنگی نجابت را
نقطه
نقطه
آب می دادند.

و اینجا چگونه به قرن لک زده
آوای تبسم ریخت؟

این جا که به پاشنه پای کوه هم
دامن میبافند
و روی آن به سنگ لحد نقش می زنند
آرامگاه خوجه انصار

ODE TO MY EARRINGS

This is for you who continually
        tremble
        whirl
        shimmy
you who are green at heart
with a slender frame—

I've reserved a place for you
on my shoulders
where you can live,
where, hey!
you can dance to every wind,
move to every tune
here on my shoulders
and sing a melody for the others.
Happiness is the color yellow—
        it shines
        it spins
even if it is night,
even if the wind is silent
and anxiety's lamp ignited.

تقدیم به گوشواره هایم

برای شما که همیشه می لرزید

می چرخید

می لولید

قلب سبز دارید

و اندام های باریک

برای شما

جا روی دوشم هست

تا زندگی کنید

هی

به هر بادی برقصید

به هر سازی پا بکوبید روی شانه هایم

و برای دیگران آواز بخوانید

خوشبختی رنگ زردی دارد

می درخشد

می چرخد

حتی اگر شب باشد

حتی اگر باد نوزد

و چراغ دلهره روشن باشد.

ROWS OF POCKMARKED HOMES

Rows of pockmarked homes down our street
motion, calling—
hey,
who stole the stones
to build a human?

نقطه چین های سرک خانه ما
دست تکان می دهند
و می پرسند
های!
چه کسی سنگ ها را برای ساختن آدم ها برد

Didn't He Come Home?

What news of the traveler—didn't he come home?
Did danger overrun him that he didn't come?
What happened between Helmand and the Hari-rud—
An open road...a Talib...blood. And he didn't come.

مسافر از سفر آیا نیامد؟
رهش شد پر خطر آیا نیامد؟
میان راه هلمند و هریرود
به طالب داد سر آیا نیامد؟

A Canvas

Face caged, the quaking bird
discerns the owl, its omen-laden stare
dripping from man's brush.

پرنده روی بند
لرزید تا تفنگ را
روی بوم نقاشی مرد دید.

PROTEST

My fingers tap the table
seven thousand seven hundred and seventy-seven times—
        my sign of protest.

It is unjust.
On Thursdays, black-cloud weather rolls in
without reason
and everyone shuts up.

***

When my own fingers dust my shoulders
with 7,777 years of regret
we can't say
it is the rain's fault.
It comes back to this.
We did not choose this table's wood,
my fingers did not arrange for the non-existence
of the neighbor's wife;
it is unjust.

***

The night that turns to Friday finds
all the rainy streets coming to dead ends
and I point five ways with five fingers,
all of them wet, and wait.
Maybe the non-existence of the neighbor's wife
is made of the same stuff
as my screams making their way
        skyward.

***

انگشتانم را به وسعت
هفت هزار و هفتصد و هفتاد و هفت
روی میز زدم به علامت
اعتراض
که های این منصفانه نیست
پنج شنبه ها بدون دلیل
هوا ابری باشد
و صدا شنیده نشد

***

وقتی هنوز گرد انگشتانم ۷۷۷۷ سال
ندامت را به دوش می کشند
گناه باران نیست
این بر می گردد به جنس میز که از ما نیست
و نیستی زن همسایه نیز دست دست انگشتانم نیست
این منصفانه نیست

***

شب که به جمعه می رسد
جاده ها بارانی به انتها می رسند
و من
که پنج جاده آن طرف تر انگشتانم را خم داده ام کنار هم
منتظرم.
شاید نیستی زن همسایه از جنس فریادهای من باشد
رو به آسمان

***

And it keeps going,
going,
going on...
How can we have returned
to the first rain?

***

When the neighbor's kid continues
to learn "b" for battlefield
and "j" for jihad,
how will we be able to breathe
through the gunpowder?

***

And it keeps going,
going,
going on...

***

In seven days' time
I searched the lines of my palms' unruly branches
for a sign that their roots had reached
a source of joy.
No sign.

What can we do?
Our days are spun from night
and we are woven dark, everyone groping
for someone's hand.

The story hasn't finished...
Non-existence keeps going,
going,
        going on...

وقتی هنوز
هنوز به پایان نرسیده
چگونه می شود
بر گردیم به اول باران

***

وقتی هنوز کودک همسایه
با سین سنگرمی کشد
و با جیم به جهاد می رود

چگونه باید نفس از باروت گرفت

***

هنوز
هنوز ادامه دارد

***

میان خطوط نا منظم دستانم
به دنبال هفت روز می گردم که ریشه دوانده باشد به خوشی هایم
که ندوانده

کاری نمی شود کرد
روزها از جنس تاریکی اند وما از جنس شب
و همه به دنبال رابطه

این آخر قصه نیست
نیست هنوز ادامه دارد
ادامه و دارد

And whether or not I exist,
it is not finished,
not yet finished.

(2009-10)

و من که باشم یا نباشم
این نیست
هنوز نیست

۱۳۸۸

ROYA SHARIFI

روىا شریفی

(1984-)

Roya Sharifi (Rūyā Sharīfī) was born in 1984 in Herat, Afghanistan. She received her bachelor's degree in Persian Literature at Herat University. Her poetry collection, called *Bū-ye Khāb: Majmua'h She'r* (*Fragrance of Dreams: A Collection of Poetry*), was published in Herat in 2009 as the sixteenth volume of the "Persian Dari Literature of Today" series by Fedāyi Herawī Press. Her poetry is also included in the four previously mentioned anthologies: *Haq bā tamāme durūgh-hā ast* (*Lies Have the Right of Way,* 2005), *Kojāhā hanūz estāda-and* (*Where Do They Now Stand?* 2008), *Īnjā chahārshanbe ast* (*It is Wednesday Here,* 2010) and *Īnjā naguftahā ast* (*There is Much Left Unsaid Here,* 2010). Sharifi often posts new poetry on her blog at http://www.boykhab.blogfa.com/

Roya Sharifi, courtesy of Roya Sharifi

Book cover of *Būy-e Khāb* by Roya Sharifi. Photo by Farzana Marie

Note on the Translations

The main surprise in Roya Sharifi's poems comes in twists of theme and meaning in the midst of highly traditional forms. Most of the poems in her collections are ghazals, with a few quatrain and free-verse variations. While many of Sharifi's ghazals treat more expected topics such as love and longing, several of them use this melodic, rhythmic form to call attention to the disruptive forces that have perpetuated conflict in her nation, critique religious hypocrites, and examine economic, social, and political issues like materialism and corruption.

In "Those Bleeding Tulips," we understand the target of her jabs to be the fundamentalist and extremist forces that have claimed Islam for their mantra but operate in ignorance, destroying the health and prosperity of a nation ("the locust-army marched en masse on rows of wheat"), with no thought for the future, for the "horizon of their history." In Dari, the name of this poem is simply *Lāla-hā* ("Tulips," also often called *Gul-e Lāla* or "Tulip-Flower"). In English, I felt the same simple title would lose too much of the inferred power associated with *Lāla* in Dari. One image that comes to mind is enormous fields of red tulips in bloom, especially in Afghanistan's north. Since it blooms in the spring, the flower has come to be associated with the celebration of the Persian New Year in March, coinciding with the spring equinox. With a national fame akin to the Rose Parade in Pasadena, CA, thousands travel to the city of Mazar-e Sharif to participate in Nauruz festivities. The bloom also invokes love, and something darker: martyrdom. While it is impossible to translate the feeling associated with this flower, "Those Bleeding Tulips" at least provides the color-association (red, for the blood of martyrs) and alludes to the desecration of the beautiful, which is central to the poem.

"Fragrance of Dreams" is perhaps the most traditional theme-wise of the poems included here. It addresses itself to a beloved who, either through absence, abandonment, or unrequited affection, has caused the speaker grief. The most likely source of grief is coldness or rejection, as suggested by the lines, "Your heart may be a salt desert yet my eyes / Follow its saline orbit awash in angst." The poem's most poignant moment comes at the end, as the speaker, a self-aware poet, confesses that she stays awake to experience the moments of greatest connection and closeness...when the cold-hearted beloved is sleeping, eyelids "awash in the fragrance of dreams." Despite the anxiety present in this poem, there is also a sense of fullness and satisfaction in it, as echoed in the repeated end-phrase, *labrīz ast* (is full of, or overflowing with). Rather than try to duplicate this form, which in this case would have been substantially tedious, I used the repeated word "awash" to draw out a similar sense of satiation.

Sharifi's poem "A Gamble" may have the most contemporary and relatable feel for English-speaking, especially American, readers, who have witnessed and experienced the most crushing economic trends in recent history. The mention of "dollar and dinar" brings to mind the stock exchange and international markets, but the piece alludes to existential issues beyond the economic. "We return to the matter of the lantern, having lost / the sun again in the shadows on the wall." The repetition of the word "lost" makes this poem reminiscent of Elizabeth Bishop's villanelle, "One Art," with its refrain, "The art of losing isn't hard to master." In translating Sharifi's piece, I kept "lost/we lost" as the driving end-word or phrase while hopefully shielding the English version from a sing-song kind of sound with a generous use of enjambment.

A GAMBLE

Whatever we had or didn't have, we inevitably lost—
all that a life amasses, in one turn, lost.
Despite the warning shout of the garden's guard we lost
the tall date palm to axe-carrying man
and where can we carry this shame?—we lost
our simpler selves to the dollar, the dinar
and from the height of valor we never actually had, we lost
our bearings, fell by accident into getting and having.
We return to the matter of the lantern, having lost
the sun again in shadows on the wall.
And woe to us, who lost the words just
as we were about to testify. Don't give us
another speech about recovering what we lost:
we are blurred with *we were* when we gambled and lost
the future in the replay in the present of the past.

(2005)

قمار

دار و ندار خود همه ناچار باختیم
یک عمر هر چه داشته یکبار باختیم
فریاد ای محافظ باغ و درخت سبز !
نخل بلند را به تبردار باختیم
این ننگ را کجا ببریم این که ساده دل
خود را چنین به دالر و دینار باختیم
ما از شهامتی که نداریم هر زمان
در گیر و دار حادثه بسیار باختیم
فانوس را دگر مطلب ز آنکه بارها
خورشید را به سایهٔ دیوار باختیم
ای وای ما که از پس عمری سکوت تلخ
فریاد را به لحظه ی اظهار باختیم
دیگر سخن ز بردن و از باختن مگو
بر ما که هست و بود به تکرار باختیم

۱۳۸۴

FRAGRANCE OF DREAMS

The liquid expanse is awash in surf
My cottage is awash in moonlight
Ask me for tonight's love-themed verse
The poet's lucid mood awash in brilliance
As night brims with luminous flames
Hand me the goblet awash in wine
Times are vile and the path to life a pyre
Your heart may be a salt desert yet my eyes
Follow its saline orbit awash in angst.
Don't tell: at times I evade sleep 'til sunrise,
long as your lids are awash in the fragrance of dreams.

بوی خواب

تمام وسعت آب از حباب لبریز است
درون کلبه ام از ماهتاب لبریز است
ز من بجو غزل عاشقانه ای امشب
که طبع شعرم از شعر ناب لبریز است
شب است و شمع فروزان و شور و شوق فزون
بده پیاله که خم از شراب لبریز است
زمانه کجرو و دون است و کوره راه حیات
چو جعد گیسویم از پیچ و تاب لبریز است
دلت اگر که کویر است چشم من اما
مدار غصه که از اشک و آب لبریز است
مگو که تا به سحر گه ز خواب بیزارم
از آن که چشم تو از بوی خواب لبریز است

THOSE BLEEDING TULIPS

They gave no quarter in those freezing nights,
only darkness, filled with laments.
First they crushed the heart's defenses,
then tore limb from every limb of tree and leaf
and gardens blooming tulips in the spring:
they marked them all for summary destruction
(amazingly in the commotion a bird broke free).
As the locust-army marched en masse on rows of wheat
without cause except for ignorance
and blind to the horizon of their history,
they filled their laps with slaughtered innocents.
Don't speak of the zeal of those bleeding tulips;
their destroyers' slogans were all *Islam* and *liberation*
but they came in anything but peace.
And now the world thinks it knows us
by the famous "valor" of the Afghan nation.

(2004)

لاله ها

نبود جز شب و شبهای سرد ظلمانی
به غیر شیون و اشک فضای حیرانی
تبر دلانه شکستند شاخ برگ درخت
و باغ و گریهٔ تلخی برای ویرانی
تمام باغ پر از لاله های پر پر بود
پرندهٔ که رها بود در پریشانی
هجوم خیل ملخ در مسیر گندمزار
دلیل هم که ندارند غیر نادانی
ندیده بود افق هیچگه به تاریخش
چنین به دامن خود قتل عام انسانی
نگو ز غیرت آن لاله های بشکسته
شعارشان همه آزادی و مسلمانی
برای جمله جهان این حقیقت است هنوز
شهامت است شهامت پیام افغانی

۱۳۸۳

SELECTED BIBLIOGRAPHY

Ahmadi, Wali. *Modern Persian Literature in Afghanistan*. Routledge, 2008. E-book.

Afzal-Khan, Fawzia. *Shattering the Stereotypes: Muslim Women Speak Out*. Northampton, MA: Olive Branch Press, 2005.

Akhtari, Fatama, with Arley Loewen. "No Right to Write, No Freedom to Sing: The Role of Afghan Women in Literature and Music." *Images of Afghanistan: Exploring Afghan Culture Through Art and Literature*. Ed. Arley Loewen and Josette McMichael. Oxford: Oxford University Press, 2011.

Anjuman, Nadia. *Gul-e Dūd-ī (Smoke-Bloom)*. Herat, Afghanistan: Herat Literary Society, 2005.

Armstrong, Sally. *Veiled Threat: The Hidden Power of the Women of Afghanistan*. New York: Penguin Putnam, Inc., 2001.

Benard, Cheryl. *Veiled Courage: Inside the Afghan Women's Resistance*. New York: Broadway, Books, 2002.

Bennet, Paula. *My Life a Loaded Gun: Female Creativity and Feminist Poetics*. Boston: Beacon Press, 1986.

Boesen, Inger W. "Conflicts of Solidarity in Pakhtun Women's Lives." *Women and Islamic Societies: Social Attitudes and Historical Perspectives*. Ed. Bo Utas. London: Curzon Press, 1983.

Caged Bird: Stories from Safe House and Poems of Nadia Anjuman. Kabul, Afghanistan: HAWCA (Humanitarian Assistance for Woman and Children of Afghanistan), 2011.

Dalrymple, William. *Return of a King: The Battle for Afghanistan, 1839-42*. New York, NY: Alfred A. Knopf, 2013.

Delloye, Isabelle. *Women of Afghanistan*. Saint Paul, MN: Ruminator Books, 2003.

Doubleday, Veronica. "Gendered Voices and Creative Expression in the Singing of Chaharbeiti Poetry in Afghanistan." *Ethnomusicology Forum*, 20.1 (2011), 3-31.

Doubleday, Veronica. *Three Women of Herat*. Austin: University of Texas Press, 1990.

Doucet, Lyse. "Dangerous 'Truth': The Kabul Women's Poetry Club." *BBC News Website*. 21 Oct 2013.

Dupree, Nancy. "Socialist Realism in the Literature of Afghanistan." *Journal of South Asian Literature*, 27.2 (1992): 85-114.

Ebrahimi, Mahbubeh. *Bādhā khwāharān-e man-and (The Winds Are My Sisters)*. Tehran: Sure Mehr, 2007.

Ehsani, Shahbaz, ed. and trans. *Mirrors and Songs: A Selection of Poetry of Afghan Women*. Lexington, KY: Self-published, 2012.

Ellis, Deborah. *Women of the Afghan War*. Westport, CT: Praeger, 2000.

Emadi, Hafizullah. *Repression, Resistance, and Women in Afghanistan*. Westport, CT: Praeger, 2002.

Fani, Aria. "Ambassadors of Life: Poetry of Afghan Women." *PBS Website: Tehran Bureau*. 10 Jun 2011.

Fani, Aria. "Daughters of Khorasan: Literary Voices of Change." *Khorasan Zameen Website*. 4 Jan 2012.

Faramanesh, Muzhgan. *Andīshahāy-e dard-ālud (Pain-Tainted Reflections)*. Herat, Afghanistan: Fedāyi Herawī Press, 2011.

Gardesh, Hafizullah. "Afghan Poet's Death Raises Many Questions." *War & Peace Reporting: The Women's Reporting & Dialogue Programme*, 15.2 (2005).

Glasse, Jennifer. "Afghan Women Reclaim Voice Through Poetry." *Al-Jazeera* Web video report. 18 May 2012.

Green, Nile, and Nushin Arbabzadah. *Afghanistan in Ink: Literature Between Diaspora and Nation*. New York: Columbia University Press, 2012.

Griswold, Eliza. "Why Afghan Women Risk Death to Write Poetry." *The New York Times*. April 27, 2012.

Griswold, Eliza and Murphy, Seamus. "Afghanistan: On Love and Suicide." *Multi-Media Web Project*. 27 April 2012.

Haidari, Fariba. *Wa āwāz-hāye benafshe beqānūn (And the Violet Tunes of Lawlessness)*. Herat, Afghanistan: Fedāyi Herawī Press, 2005.

Heath, Jennifer and Zahedi, Ashraf, ed. *Land of the Unconquerable: The Lives of Contemporary Afghan Women*. Berkeley and Los Angeles: University of California Press, 2011.

Hopkirk, Peter. *The Great Game: The Struggle for Empire in Central Asia*. New York: Kodansha International, 1992.

Jahangiri, Ghuissou and Rooholamin Amini, ed. Khalil Rostamkhani, trans. (Bilingual book) *Simorgh, The Thirty Wise Birds: An Anthology of Poems and Photographs for Peace in Afghanistan*. Afghanistan: Armanshahr Foundation, 2010.

Jahangiri, Ghuissou, ed. *Zanān solh ra mīsurāyand, (Women Celebrate Peace: An Anthology of Poems)*. Herat, Afghanistan: Armanshahr Foundation, 2009.

Kojāhā hanūz estāda-and (Where Do They Now Stand?). Herat, Afghanistan: Ahmad Shah Massoud Foundation, 2008.

Lamb, Christina. *The Sewing Circles of Herat: My Afghan Years*. London: HarperCollins, 2002.

"Landays." *Poetry* 202:3, June, 2013 (Entire Issue).

Logan, Harriet. *Unveiled: Voices of Women in Afghanistan*. New York: Regan Books, 2002.

Majrouh, Sayd Bahodine, ed. *Songs of Love and War: Afghan Women's Poetry*. Trans. Marjolijn de Jager. New York: Other Press, 2003.

Mahajer, Najaf 'Ali. *Farhangnameh-e zanan-e parsiguy* (Dictionary of Persian-Speaking Women). Tehran: Avahdi, 2004.

Milani, Farzaneh. *Veils and Words: The Emerging Voices of Iranian Women Writers*. Syracuse, NY: Syracuse University Press, 1992.

Milani, Farzaneh. *Words, Not Swords: Iranian Women Writers and the Freedom of Movement*. Syracuse, NY: Syracuse University Press, 2011.

Millet, J.B. Co. Oriental Series Vol XVIII: *Afghanistan*. Norwood, MA: The Plimpton Press, 1910.

Mills, Margaret A. "Gender and Verbal Performance Style in Afghanistan." *Gender, Genre and Power in South Asian Expressive Traditions*. Ed. Arjun Appadurai, Frank Korom, and Margaret Mills. Philadelphia: Pennsylvania University Press, 1991. 56-77.

Mirshahi, Masood, ed. and Leila Enayat-Seraj, trans. *She'r-e zanān-e Afghanistan* (The Hidden Face of Afghan Women: Poetess Women of Afghanistan). Paris: Khavaran, 2000.

Mirzahi, Zakiyeh. "She'r-e zanan-e Afghanestan" (Afghanistan Women's Poetry). *Bokhara* 44 (2006): 337-339.

Mohammadi, Reza. "Zanān-e shā'er-e sunnat-shekan" (Tradition-Breaking Women Poets). *Jadid Online*. 2006.

Naderi, Partaw. "Literature in the Course of Politics in Afghanistan." *Tajikam* Website. 2007-2011.

Najimi, Abdul Wasay. *Herat, The Islamic City: A Study in Conservation.* London: Curzon Press, 1975.

Nazemi, Latif. "A Look at Persian Literature in Afghanistan." Tajikam Website. 2007-2011.

Noorzayi, Fereshta Nilab Sahel. *Widā' (Farewell)*. Herat, Afghanistan: Fruzān Bārez, 2010.

Olszewska, Zuzanna. "'A Desolate Voice:' Poetry and Identity among Young Afghan Refugees in Iran." *Iranian Studies. Special Issue: Afghan Refugees* 40.2 (2007): 203-224.

Olszewska, Zuzanna. "Stealing the Show: Women Writers at an Afghan Literary Festival in Tehran." September 2005/Sharivar 1383. www.badjens.com/afghan.lit.html

Olszewska, Zuzanna. "A Hidden Discourse: Afghanistan's Women Poets." *Land of the Unconquerable: The Lives of Contemporary Afghan Women*. Ed. Jennifer Heath and Ashraf Zahedi, Berkeley: University of California Press, 2011.

Omrani, Bijan and Leeming, Matthew. *Afghanistan: A Companion and Guide*. New York, NY: Odyssey Books and Guides, 2005.

Ramish, Somaia. *Kamī barāye khudam (A Little Bit for Me)* Herat, Afghanistan: Fedāyi-e Herawī Press, 2008.

Ramish, Somaia. *Dar parāntaz: guft wa shunīd-e Somaia Rāmish bā chehra-hāy-e farhangī-e Herāt. (In Parenthesis: Interviews by Somaia Ramish with Herat's Cultural Figures).* Herat, Afghanistan: Fedāyi-e Herawī Press, 2010.

Ramish, Somaia. *Yak Fasl-e Khāb-e Anār (A Season of Pomegranate Dreams).* Herat, Afghanistan: Naw-Andīshān Cultural, Social Organization, 2013.

Rasekh, Shapour, ed. *Hamzabani wa Hamdili (One Tongue, One Heart: Selected Poems of Some Contemporary Afghan Poets).* Jabbari, 2012.

Rostam-Povey Elah. "Afghan Refugees in Iran, Pakistan, the U.K. and the U.S and Life after Return." *Iranian Studies. Special Issue: Afghan Refugees* 40.2 (2007): 241-261.

Rostamy-Povey, Elaheh. *Afghan Women: Identity and Invasion.* London: Zed Books, Ltd, 2007.

Rostami, Povey E. "Women in Afghanistan: Passive Victims of the Borga or Active Social Participants?"*Development in Practice.* 13 (2003): 266-277.

Saeed, Zohra and Muradi, Sahar, ed. *One Story, Thirty Stories: An Anthology of Contemporary Afghan American Literature.* Fayetteville, AR: University of Arkansas Press, 2010.

Sahel, Elaha. *Khoshbakhtī rang-e zardi dārad (Happiness is the Color Yellow).* Herat, Afghanistan. Fedāyi Herawī Press, 2010.

Sharifi, Roya. *Bū-ye Khāb (Fragrance of Dreams).* Herat, Afghanistan: Fedāyi Herawī Press, 2009.

Shalinsky, Audrey C. "Reason, Desire, and Sexuality: The Meaning of Gender in Northern Afghanistan." *Ethos* 14.4 (1986): 323-343.

Sikorsky, Radek. *Dust of the Saints: A Journey to Herat in a Time of War.* Lodon: Chatto & Windus, 1989.

Skaine, Rosemarie. *The Women of Afghanistan Under the Taliban.* Jefferson, NC: McFarland & Co., Inc., Publishers, 2002.

Skaine, Rosemarie. *Afghanistan in the Post-Taliban Era: How Lives Have Changed and Where They Stand Today.* Jefferson, NC: McFarland & Co., Inc., Publishers, 2008.

Stack, Shannon Carline. *Herat: A Political and Social Study.* Dissertation. University of California, Los Angeles, 1975.

Subtelny, Maria E. "Scenes from the Literary Life of Timurid Herat." *Logos Islamikos: Studia Islamica in Honorem Georgii Michaelis Wickens.* Ed. Roger M.

Savory and Dionisius A. Agius. Toronto: Pontifical Institute of Mediaeval Studies, 1984. 137-155.

Tabibi, Abdulhakim. *Tārikh-e mukhtasar-e Herāt dar asr-e Tīmūryān.* Tehran: Enteshaaraate Hirmand, 1989 (1368).

Talattof, Kamran. *The Politics of Writing in Iran: A History of Modern Persian Literature.* Syracuse, NY: Syracuse University Press, 2000.

Talattof, Kamran. *Modernity, Sexuality and Ideology in Iran: The Life and Legacy of a Popular Female Artist.* Syracuse, NY: Syracuse University Press, 2011.

Tober, Diane. "My Body is Broken Like my Country': Identity, Nation and Repatriation Among Afghan Refugees in Iran." *Iranian Studies. Special Issue: Afghan Refugees* 40:2 (2007): 263-285.

Vanzan, Anna. "The Double Exile: The Poetry of Afghan Women Refugees in Iran." *El Ghibli Rivista Online di Letteratura Della Migrazione.* 5: 22. December 2008.

Webster, Rachel with Zuzanna Olszewska, "Nadia Anjuman (1980-2005)." *UniVerse, A United Nations of Poetry* Website, 2013.

Widmark, Anders. "The View From Within: An Introduction to New Afghan Literature." *Words Without Borders* Website, May 2011.

Wolfe, Nancy Hatch. *Herat: A Pictoral Guide*. Kabul, Afghanistan: The Afghan Tourist Organization, 1966.

Youth Club of Herat Literary Society, ed. *Haq bā tamāme durūgh-hā ast: Majmu'aye She'r* (*Lies Have the Right of Way: A Poetry Anthology*). Herat, Afghanistan: Herat Literary Society, 2005.

Youth Club of Herat Literary Society, ed. *Ïnjā chahārshanbe ast* (*It Is Wednesday Here*): *A Poetry Anthology*. Herat, Afghanistan: Herat Literary Society, 2010.

Youth Club of Herat Literary Society, ed. *Ïnjā naguftahā ast* (*There is Much Left Unsaid Here*): *A Poetry Anthology*. Herat, Afghanistan: Fedāyi Herawī Press, spring 2010.

ABOUT THE AUTHOR

FARZANA MARIE grew up nomadically in Chile, California, and Kazakhstan, to later spend years in Afghanistan as a civilian volunteer, Air Force officer, and scholar. She is a PhD candidate at the University of Arizona's School of Middle Eastern and North African Studies, where she focuses on Persian Literature with a minor in Creative Writing. She holds a B.S. in Humanities from the U.S. Air Force Academy and an M.A. in English from the University of Massachusetts, Boston. Farzana served on active duty for over six years, including two consecutive years deployed in Afghanistan (2010-2012), where she also worked as a civilian volunteer at Kabul orphanages in 2003 and 2004. She is author of the nonfiction book, *Hearts for Sale! A Buyer's Guide to Winning in Afghanistan* (Worldwide Writings, 2013), and the poetry chapbook, *Letters to War and Lethe* (Finishing Line Press, 2014). Farzana serves as president of the nonprofit corporation she co-founded, Civil Vision International. She has a vision for crossing boundaries toward connection, healing, and transformation through literature and the arts. You can find her at *www.farzanamarie.com* or on Twitter *@farzanamarie*.

CPSIA information can be obtained
at www.ICGtesting.com
Printed in the USA
JSHW051602130920
7849JS00003B/9